MATH REVIEW TOOLKIT

GARY L. LONG

Virginia Polytechnic Institute
and State University

CHEMISTRY
THE CENTRAL SCIENCE

Brown ▲ LeMay ▲ Bursten
EIGHTH EDITION

PRENTICE HALL
Upper Saddle River, NJ 07458

Senior Editor: John Challice
Special Projects Manager: Barbara A. Murray
Production Editor: Mark Marsden
Supplement Cover Manager: Paul Gourhan
Supplement Cover Designer: Liz Nemeth
Manufacturing Manager: Trudy Pisciotti

Printed in the United States of America

10 9 8 7 6 5 4 3 2

ISBN 0-13-084103-X

Prentice-Hall International (UK) Limited, London
Prentice-Hall of Australia Pty. Limited, Sydney
Prentice-Hall Canada, Inc., Toronto
Prentice-Hall Hispanoamericana, S.A., Mexico
Prentice-Hall of India Private Limited, New Delhi
Prentice-Hall (Singapore) Pte. Ltd.
Prentice-Hall of Japan, Inc., Tokyo
Editora Prentice-Hall do Brazil, Ltda., Rio de Janeiro

Contents

Preface
To The Student

Y our study of General Chemistry will require skills of memorization, basic logic, and mathematics. Having taught thousands of students General Chemistry, I find the stumbling block for many has been mathematics. Regardless of how many facts and equations you have memorized, your mastery of mathematics is paramount to your success in general chemistry. These skills are not new abilities you must master. They are the math skills of algebra and trigonometry that you learned in high school. Calculus is not required for your study of General Chemistry.

It is the purpose of this booklet to guide you through the mathematics that are used in your text. The math skills for each chapter are outlined and examples are worked. References are made to worked examples in your text and similar chapter problems.

The case of a life sciences student planted the idea for this little book. This young man was going around for the seventh time in General Chemistry. He could never manage to pass the first test so he would drop out and wait until the next semester to try again. Fortunately, he came to me at the beginning of the course. He was desperate; he could not graduate until he passed chemistry. After speaking with him, I found his limitation was not inadequate math training, but a basic fear of math and science. He would "freeze up" on the math problems on the exam. During the semester I met with the student and explained how to perform these calculations using the methods that are described in this booklet. The student successfully completed the course with a B average.

Although we cannot absolutely guarantee your success in chemistry with the use of this booklet, mastery of the material presented here will greatly help you. If you are not sure how your skills rate, take a few moments and complete the *"Self Test for Math Skills"* in Section 15 of this booklet. It will help you assess your skills.

Chemistry is an exciting field of study that touches every area of our lives. It is our hope that this booklet will help you discover this excitement by demystifying the mathematical principles involved in General Chemistry.

Gary L. Long

long@vt.edu

The first year of college is a major balancing act. Study and fun, what ratio? Your college courses will require more than twice the preparation and study time of high school, so learn to make wise use of your time.

Fear inhibits our ability to reason. One of the most brilliant young men I know tells me what separates his performance from others is that he doesn't stop when he becomes frustrated. At the wall of *frustration* most people give up. *Persistence* is important.

Many college students have been forced to change their career dreams because they could not make it through General Chemistry. This unpleasantness does not give chemistry a good name nor does it give chemistry professors an easy grace at social functions when asked their occupation. Some of you may need to change your career option to a different discipline for which you are gifted. As a student at Wake Forest University, a very kind English professor pointed this out to me at a time when Organic Chemistry was causing me great distress. Time is too valuable to spend it in the wrong place. However, for those of you heading in the right direction, we do not want chemistry to be a stumbling block for your dreams.

We hope that your experience with chemistry will be a victorious one and that in some small way this booklet will make a difference. Write us and tell us your stories as well as your triumphs.

Sharon D. Long

sdlong@vt.edu

Section 1

Your Calculator and Its Functions

A recent Peanuts cartoon displays Snoopy holding up a calculator with the expression, "I don't need to think, I have batteries..." This statement is far from reality in any study that requires the use of mathematics. Calculators are invaluable tools when working with long equations and involved calculations. What you can do in a few seconds on your calculator now would have taken a chemistry student 20 years ago several minutes to do by hand. Even with this greater potential speed in problem solving, you have to set up the equations before you use the calculator. Besides writing the equations down on paper, you may have to rearrange them so that you can use your calculator's functions to solve the problem. You will need to become acquainted with your calculator so you will know how to properly set up the problem. The mastery of the equations and your calculator's operation will allow you to get these "speedy" answers.

In your general chemistry course you will encounter problems using arithmetic operations (addition, subtraction, multiplication, and division), trigonometric operations (cos, sin, $\cos^{-1}$, and $\sin^{-1}$), and logarithmic operations (log, ln, 10^x, e^x, powers and roots). You will also deal with exponential notation in many of these problems. In the following sections, we will discuss these functions and how to use your calculator to solve problems in General Chemistry.

1.1 Arithmetic Operations

These operations are generally straightforward. To add two numbers we enter the first number, press the [+] key, enter the second number and press the [=] key. The sum of the numbers should appear on the display.

Some calculators may not follow this sequence because they are designed to use Reverse Polish Notation, RPN. These types of calculators do not have an [=] key. Calculations are performed by first entering the numbers into memory "stacks" on the calculator and then pressing the desired key. Although this method seems horribly backward at first, the use of RPN can be quite advantageous in dealing with calculations contained within a large formula.

1.2 Trigonometric Operations

You will encounter several equations in chemistry that will use the trigonometric operations of sin and cos. The process of determining the sin or cos of an angle is similar for conventional and RPN calculators. To determine the sin of 30°, enter 30 into the calculator and depress the [sin] key. The value of 0.50 should appear. *Note: It is most important that your calculator is in the "degree" mode and not in "radian" or "grd" when performing these calculations.*

Other calculations will require you to determine what degree value in sin x will correspond to a certain value, say $0.60 = \sin x$. You can determine this x by using one of several keys on your calculator. Look for the [sin^{-1}] or [arcsin] key. Enter the value of 0.60 and then depress the [sin^{-1}], or the [arcsin] key. A value of 36.9° should appear on the display. The use of this function may require you to first depress a [2nd], [INV], [f], or [g] key.

1.3 Logarithmic Functions

These functions will include the use of log, 10^x, ln, and e^x. Also to be discussed in this section are roots and powers.

In calculations involving logarithmic relationships, there are two different mathematical bases that are used. On your calculator you will find base 10 logarithmic functions, [10^x] and [log], and base$_e$ functions, [e^x] and [ln]. These logarithmic functions are not the same. Base$_{10}$ math is structured around examining the properties of raising the number 10 to different powers, while base$_e$ math is structured on using 2.71828.... You will find that many calculations, such as thermodynamic relationships, are defined using log, not ln. Part of this reasoning is historical, due to the fact that calculations involving base$_{10}$ math are much easier for people to work with than base$_e$ mathematics.

Many of these relationships were developed and refined by chemists before the advent of the computer and pocket calculator. For this reason the base$_{10}$ approach was favored. As an example, consider the calculation of the log of 1,000. Here, we must figure out to what power 10 must be raised to equal 1,000. We know from our algebra training that if we cube 10, we should obtain 1,000. The calculation of ln (1,000), which involves base$_e$, is another matter. To determine this value we must use the calculator. We first enter 1,000 and then press the [ln] key. The value of 6.908 should appear on the display.

The calculations of 10^x and e^x are sometimes referred to as anti-logs in calculator manuals. Most calculators have a [10^x] and an [e^x] key. Some models may require you to press the [INV] key to use an anti-log function. In this scheme of thinking [e^x] = [INV] [ln]. To determine $e^{1.5}$, enter 1.5 into the calculator and depress the [e^x] or the [INV] [ln] key(s). A value of 4.5 should appear on the display.

Powers and roots are another important use of the calculator in chemistry. All calculators possess square root [$\sqrt{x}$] and square keys [x^2]. The use of these functions is straightforward. However, you may need to determine cubic (and higher) roots in your studies. Your calculator may have a [y^x] key that will enable you to determine these roots as well as to calculate a number raised to a power. To determine the roots with the [y^x] it is necessary to enter the root as the value of $1/x$. To find the cubic root of 77, enter 77 into the calculator (as the y value), enter 1/3 (as the x value), and depress the [y^x] key. You should see the value of 4.3 on the display.

Don't be discouraged if your calculator does not have a [y^x] key. If it has a [log] and a [10^x] or [INV] [ln] key(s), you can determine any root of a number. To calculate the cubic root of 77:

- enter 77 as the y value
- use the [log] button (1.8864 will be displayed)
- divide the result by 3, the xth root, (0.6288 will be displayed)
- press the [10^x] button on the quotient (4.254 will be displayed)
- the result (4.3) is the cube root of 77

This method should allow you to take the nth root of any number that you may encounter in your studies in chemistry. For instance, try computing the fourth root of 1.9×10^{-11}. The log of this number is -10.72. Dividing this number by 4 and taking the anti-log yields the answer 2.1×10^{-3}. This method will be useful to you in Chapter 17 where you will be determining the solubility of salts.

1.4 Exponential Notation and Your Calculator

Exponential notation is a method used to express very large and very small numbers on your calculator. These numbers are expressed by multiplying the significant portion of the number by a multiplier based on 10^x.

To use the exponential notation feature on your calculator, you will use a [sci], [exp] or [EE] function. Consider the process of entering 1.6×10^{-17}. First enter the significant portion of 1.6 into the display. Next press the [sci] or equivalent key and enter the number 17. You will need to change the sign of the power of 17 (which should appear in the right hand portion of the display), so press the [+/-] key to cause the power to read -17. Depending on the type of calculator you have, you may need to press the [=] key to end the sequence.

You will also be able on your calculator to convert from regular notation to exponential notation. If the number 1,000,000 was in the display of your calculator, you could depress the [sci] then [=] keys to cause the number to appear in exponential notation (1.000×10^6) on the display.

Please be aware that different calculators may require different methods for the entering of numbers in exponential notation or the conversion of numbers to and from exponential notation. As trite as it may seem, you may need to consult the manual that came with your calculator. I have done this on more than one occasion for the various calculators I use.

More information on exponential notation and its use in chemical calculations can be found in Appendix A of your textbook.

1.5 Choosing A Calculator

There are many excellent brands of calculators on the market available to the chemistry student. If you have not yet purchased a calculator, consider the following questions.

- Will you be pursuing a science, business, or liberal arts degree?
- Do you need a programmable or graphing calculator?

The calculator that you need in this course must be able to perform the basic functions in addition to trigonometric and logarithmic functions. It must support exponential notation. Prices of "scientific" calculators usually start at $15.

With regards to the first question, if you are planning to pursue a field of study in the liberal arts, the above mentioned calculator would well suit your needs. Science majors may wish to consider a calculator that contains a statistical analysis package and programmability in addition to the basic functions. Business majors would be well advised to purchase the basic "scientific" calculators. The calculations that you would use in later business courses will require you to use specific formulas and functions that are programmed into "business" calculators.

Programmability on a calculator is a wonderful feature that allows you to quickly solve repetitive calculations that are employed in science and engineering fields. Unfortunately, programmability adds to the cost of a calculator. Models that graph mathematical functions on a small LCD screen are also becoming popular, but at a higher cost. If you are operating on a restricted budget, choose a basic "scientific" model and upgrade later to a programmable or graphing model.

After you have answered these questions, examine the brands that would meet your calculating and financial needs. Examine the calculators for the size of the display and buttons (and their spacing) on the keypad. You want a calculator that has an easy to read display and that is easy to use. In order to put more "full feature functions" some manufacturers have down-sized the keys and put three to four functions on the same key. If the keypad legend is not well designed, these types of calculators can be difficult to use.

A final factor to consider is the power source. Solar powered calculators are great while working in well lighted areas. Unfortunately, these calculators may not work well in some large lecture halls because of insufficient room lighting. However, some calculators have dual power sources: solar and battery. With this type of design, your batteries will power the calculator if the light levels are too weak. (This is especially good to know before you take your first chemistry test.)

Your calculator can be a valuable tool to you in your study of general chemistry. Take the time to acquaint yourself with its capabilities.

Section 2
Skills for Chapter 1: Introduction

2.1 Significant Figures

Every measurement that is made in the laboratory is subject to error. The level of this error (or certainty) depends upon the instruments used in the measurement and the skill of the person performing the operations. Even if we can eliminate the systematic errors (*i.e.* miscalibration of the pan balance) we will still encounter random errors in lab. These random errors will determine the accuracy of our measurement.

Rather than stating the error with each number a chemist may use in a calculation, the practice of using "significant figures" in calculations is employed. The significant figures of a number can be thought of as those digits in the number that do not change when the uncertainty is factored in. (The rules used for determining the number of significant figures in an expressed value are listed in Section 1.5 of your textbook.) As an example of the effect of uncertainty on the number of significant figures, consider the food sample which was found to have 1.33 mg of Ca per serving with an error of 0.1 mg for the determination. Based on the uncertainty we should only say that the sample contains 1.3 mg of Ca. The number has only 2 significant figures. It is of no importance to attempt to convey that the calculation indicated a second 3 (i.e. 1.3<u>3</u>) in the decimal. The error made this digit "insignificant".

You will be asked in this course to use significant figures in the estimation of answers to your calculations. As an example, consider the problem of determining the circumference of a cylinder. With a simple ruler you could determine the diameter to be 2.5 inches. From the relationship of $C = \pi \times d$, you could use your calculator to determine the circumference, C. The display of the calculator would read (7.853981...). What value do you report? What is significant?

The basic rule is that you report your answer using the least number of significant figures. In the multiplicative operation above,

the diameter was only reported to two significant figures. The answer
should be reported as 7.9 in.

Rules for addition and subtraction are slightly different. Consider
adding a 0.001 g weight to an object resting on a pan balance and
indicating a value of 23.2 g in mass. The addition of 0.001 to 23.2
would yield a theoretical answer of 23.201 g. However, if the pan
balance used had an error of 0.1 g, the addition of 0.001 g to this
weight would be insignificant. The uncertainty will limit our ability to
express accurately the sum of the combined weights. Sample Exercises
1.6 and 1.7 show worked problems on significant figures. Problems
1.33-1.38 address the use of significant figures in calculations.

2.2   Exponential Notation

The calculations that you will use in this course will involve those
numbers that are exceedingly large or small. In order that you may
perform the calculations (let alone write them on one sheet of paper)
exponential notation is employed. As mentioned in your text,
exponential notation is a way to express these numbers by reducing
the number to a significant portion (discussed above) and a multiplier
based on 10^x. The metric system takes advantage of this system in
allowing us to express small masses such as nanograms (1×10^{-9}
grams) to larger masses such as kilograms (1×10^3 grams).

The use of exponential notation in equations also allows us to
quickly estimate the answer to problems involving multiplication and
division. For multiplication we sum the powers of the values
multiplied to obtain the power of the final answer. Consider the
equation:

$$x = (1.00 \times 10^3) \times (2.00 \times 10^6)$$

The product of the significant portion is 2.00. The sum of 3 and 6 is
9. For this problem

$$x = 2.00 \times 10^9$$

Division is based upon the subtraction of powers. For the problem:

$$x = \frac{6.00 \times 10^5}{2.00 \times 10^9}$$

The quotient of the significant portion is 3.00. The difference in powers is 4. By inspection, the answer to this problem is 3.00×10^{-4}.

This method of inspection can be a powerful tool. Let's say we wish to convert 1000 ft (1.000×10^3 ft) into millimeters. From the conversion table on the inside back cover of your textbook, we can find that 1 inch is equal to 25.4 mm. Since there are twelve inches in one foot, 1 ft equals 12 times this value (304.8 mm/ft or 3.048×10^2 mm/ft). If we set up the problem correctly,

$$x \text{ mm} = (1.000 \times 10^3 \text{ ft}) \times (3.048 \times 10^2 \text{ mm/ft})$$
$$x \text{ mm} = 3.048 \times 10^5 \text{mm}$$

Remember when multiplying we can sum the powers to see that the answer will be in the 10^5 range. The product of the significant portion is 3.048. The answer to this question then is there are 3.048×10^5 mm in 1000 ft or 304,800 mm in 1000 ft.

This solution did not require an electronic calculator. The key to the mental calculation lies in the inspection of the powers and the estimation of the product and the significant portion of the two values. It should be noted that before an answer can be determined, the units in the problem must be inspected. The final answer must appear in mm. The units of ft canceled by appearing both in the numerator and the denominator. If your inspection of the set up problem does not reduce to the desired units, the constants chosen or basic set up is wrong. This topic is further discussed in your textbook in Section 1.6, Dimensional Analysis.

A final example of exponential notation concerns a problem that you will encounter in Chapter 6 of your textbook where you will determine the energy of a photon. If a HeNe laser has a wavelength of 632.8 nm, what is the energy in J of a single photon? The answer is calculated using $E = hc/\lambda$, where h and c are constants and λ is the wavelength in meters. We can quickly estimate the energy by expressing all numbers in exponential notation and setting up the problem. Using this, we can write:

$$h = 6.6262 \times 10^{-34} \text{ J-s}$$
$$c = 2.997925 \times 10^8 \text{ m/s}$$
$$\lambda = 632.8 \text{ nm or } 632.8 \times 10^{-9}\text{m}$$

or 6.328×10^{-7} m

The problem can be set up to solve for E as:

$$E = (6.626 \times 10^{-34} \text{ J-s}) \times \frac{2.997925 \times 10^8\text{m/s}}{6.328 \times 10^{-7}\text{m}}$$

By inspection the power of the multiplication reduces to -26 (-34 + 8 = -26). Now looking at the power involved in the division step, we see that the -26 is in the numerator while -7 is in the denominator. The subtraction of the denominator power yields -19 (-26 - -7 = -19). From looking at the unit of the equation, we can see the first guess would place us up in the range of 10^{-19} J. By inspecting the significant portion we could estimate that $6.6 \times 3 / 6.3$ is roughly 3.1. Therefore, we could approximate the answer as 3.1×10^{-19} J. (The calculator would allow us to find that there are 3.139×10^{-19} J/photon, based on 4 significant figures.)

For more information on exponential notation, see Appendix A of your textbook. Sample Examples can be found there. Also, Chapter 1 problems 1.18, 1.19, 1.20, 1.38, 1.41 and 1.42 use exponential notation in the expression of units and measure.

2.3   Mean and Standard Deviation

If your calculator has a statistical analysis package, you may be able to calculate the mean ($\bar{x}$) and standard deviation (s) of a data set. These values are helpful in determining the accuracy and precision of your measurements.

Let us say that you have titrated five equal volumes of an unknown acid with a standard base. You have dispensed the following volume of titrant in the 5 runs: 43.8 mL, 43.30 mL, 44.10 mL, 43.90 mL and 43.70 mL. We would first enter the five values into the memory of the calculator. After final entry, we would depress the button to give us the mean, $\bar{x}$. The value of 43.76 should appear. Next, we would calculate the standard deviation, s, by pressing the appropriate buttons (s, s_x, or σ). A value of 0.30 should appear. Based on your titrating skills you could say you dispensed 43.76 +/- 0.30 mL per titration in this data set. Considering the error in the data (0.30 mL) expressing a value beyond the tenths of mL (0.1 mL) would not be significant. The correct answer should be 43.8 ± 0.3 mL, where only 3 significant figures are used.

Section 3
Chapters 3 & 4 Skills: Stoichiometry

Goals: to calculate yields, concentrations, dilutions, and titrations
Skills: multiplication and division

3.1 Yields

Part of your studies dealing with chemicals and their reactivity will be to determine the yield of a reaction. From your readings concerning stoichiometry, if we write the equation,

$$A + B \rightarrow C$$

we understand if 1 mol of A and 1 mol of B are allowed to react under favorable conditions, 1 mol of C should be produced. The *theoretical yield* of the reaction is 1 mol of C. This value could be expressed in grams instead of moles by multiplying the theoretical yield of 1 mol by the molar mass of the compound C.

Note that yield depends on the stoichiometry of the reaction. If the reaction were instead,

$$2A \rightarrow B$$

and 1 mol of A was placed in the reaction vessel, the theoretical yield would be 0.5 mol of B. Using Dimensional Analysis (Section 1.6 of your text) the theoretical yield could be found.

$$x \text{ mol} = 1 \text{ mol A} \times \frac{1 \text{ mol B}}{2 \text{ mol A}}$$

$$x \text{ mol} = 0.5 \text{ mol B}$$

In practice, the mol quantity of product that is obtained from the reaction is less than the theoretical value. The amount of product that is obtained is termed the *actual yield*.

A method in which the efficiency of a reaction is gauged is the calculation of the *percent yield*. It is defined as

$$percent\ yield = \left(\frac{actual\ yield}{theoretical\ yield}\right) \times 100\%$$

For the first reaction, if we had obtained 0.8 mol of C, the % yield would be

$$percent\ yield = \left(\frac{0.8\ mol}{1\ mol}\right) \times 100\%$$

$$percent\ yield = 80\%$$

The percent yield calculations can also be performed using the grams of actual product obtained as compared to the theoretical gram yield.

In many cases, the scientist may wish to predict the actual yield for a well characterized reaction. For instance, if the percent yield of a synthetic reaction is 90%, the actual yield may be found by multiplying the percent yield by the theoretical yield. (Remember to divide the percent yield by 100% in order to remove the % unit from the expression.) Example 3.18 uses this approach to determine the actual yield of a reaction. Additional problems are 3.79 and 3.80.

3.2 Molarity

The molarity, M, is the term that expresses the mol quantity of a dissolved substance (solute) per liter of solution. A solution that is 1.00 M NaCl contains 1.00 mol of NaCl per 1.00 L of solution. This same solution contains 58.4 g of NaCl per 1.00 L of solution.

Calculations that involve molarity will usually begin with statement of the gram quantities of solute dissolved in a quantity (mL or L) of solution. By definition,

$$M \ = \ \frac{\text{mol of solute}}{\text{L of solution}} \ = \ \frac{\left(\dfrac{\text{g of solute}}{\text{MW of solute}}\right)}{\text{L of solution}}$$

For instance, to calculate the molarity of a solution that is 10.0 g of NaCl in 400 mL of water, we would write:

$$M \ = \ \frac{\left(\dfrac{10.0 \text{ g}}{58.4 \text{ g}/\text{mol}}\right)}{0.400 \text{ L}}$$

We will first solve the numerator of the problem for the mol amount of NaCl present in the solution. If we divide 10.0 g by 58.4 g/mol, we should obtain a value of 0.171 mol NaCl. Substituting into the equation

$$M \ = \ \frac{0.171 \text{ mol}}{0.400 \text{ L}}$$

$$M = 0.428 \text{ mol NaCl} / \text{L of solution}$$

Note: It is most important to express the volume of solution only in L. Sample Exercise 4.9 and Problems 4.51 and 4.52 in your textbook for similar problems.

You may find it necessary in your work to determine what amount of solute, expressed in grams, would result in a certain molarity of solution. Consider what gram amount of NaCl is necessary to create a 0.60 M solution that is 750 mL in volume. First, let's fill the given information into the molarity expression.

$$0.60 \text{ M} \ = \ \frac{\left(\dfrac{x \text{ g}}{58.4 \text{ g}/\text{mol}}\right)}{0.750 \text{ L}}$$

To solve for x, we must cross multiply several factors in order to arrange the equation for x.

$$(0.60 \text{ M}) (0.750 \text{ L}) = \frac{x \text{ g}}{58.4 \text{ g/mol}}$$

$$(0.60 \text{ mol/L}) (0.750 \text{ L}) (58.4 \text{ g/mol}) = x \text{ g}$$

$$x \text{ g} = 26.3 \text{ g of NaCl}$$

Note that all units on the left hand side of the equation reduced to g (remember that M is in mol/L). By taking time with your cross multiplication step, the problem can be solved. This example is similar to Sample Exercises 4.10 and 4.11, and Problems 4.53 and 4.54 of your textbook.

3.3 Dilution

Dilution involves reducing the concentration of a solution by adding more solvent. Typically, a volume of solution is taken and added to a volume of solvent. Consider the dilution of a 3.00 M NaCl solution by pipetting 10.0 mL into a 1.000 L flask and filling the flask to the calibration mark with pure water. Here we are adding roughly 990 mL of water to the solution.

We can calculate the concentration of a diluted solution using the definition of molarity and Dimension Analysis (Section 1.6 of your text). Alternatively, we can use the equation

$$M_{final} = M_{initial} \times \frac{V_{initial}}{V_{final}}$$

where M_{final} is the final concentration of the diluted solution, $M_{initial}$ is the initial concentration of the concentrated solution, V_{final} is the final concentration of the diluted solution, and $V_{initial}$ is the initial concentration of the solution. For our problem, $M_{initial} = 3.00 \text{ M}$ NaCl, $V_{initial} = 10.0 \text{ mL}$, and $V_{final} = 1.000 \text{ L}$ (or 1,000 mL). Substituting these numbers into the equation, we write

$$M_{final} = 3.00 \text{ M} \times \frac{10.0 \text{ mL}}{1000 \text{ mL}}$$

$$M_{final} = 0.0300 \; M$$

Note that the volume units in a dilution calculation must be the same no matter how they are stated in the problem. Use the Dimensional Analysis scheme to check your units before reporting your answers. See Sample Exercise 4.12 for a similar problem.

The dilution equation can also be used to solve for $V_{initial}$, if the other variables of the equation are known. For instance, what volume ($V_{initial}$) of a 1.00 M solution of NaOH ($M_{initial}$) must be added to a beaker and diluted to 500.0 mL (V_{final}) in order to produce a diluted solution of 0.2500 M NaOH (M_{final}). Rearrangement of the dilution equation by cross-multiplication and division yields

$$V_{initial} = V_{final} \times \frac{M_{final}}{M_{initial}}$$

from which $V_{initial}$ can be found. Problems 4.59 and 4.60 are similar to this worked example.

3.4 Titration

Another calculation for solutions that involves cross multiplication and division is titration. As discussed in your textbook, this process involves reacting a standard solution with an unknown solution for the purpose of determining the concentration of the unknown solution. In the lab, the commonly used titrations involve acid-base reactions, precipitation reactions, redox reactions and complexation reactions.

Before any titration can be carried out, the solution stoichiometry must be known. Specifically, we must know how many moles of the titrant (standard solution) will react with the unknown. Using the simple acid-base reaction listed below, the mathematics for a titration can be set up.

$$HCl(aq) + NaOH(aq) \rightarrow H_2O(l) + NaCl(aq)$$

This reaction has a stoichiometry of 1 mol of acid to 1 mol of base. We can then write:

$$mol_{acid} = mol_{base}$$

Substituting the expression of $mol = M \times V$, we obtain:

$$M_{acid} \times V_{acid} = M_{base} \times V_{base}$$

Consider a titration of an unknown NaOH solution with a standardized HCl solution. To 50.0 mL of the unknown contained in a flask, approximately 33.8 mL of a 0.175 M standardized HCl solution was added to the flask to reach the equivalence point. From this information, we want to find out the molarity of the unknown solution.

If we rearrange the above equation by cross multiplication and division, we can solve for the molarity of the unknown base, M_{base}. Doing so yields:

$$M_{base} = \frac{M_{acid} \times V_{acid}}{V_{base}}$$

Putting in the data, we find:

$$M_{base} = \frac{0.175 \text{ mol/L} \times 0.0338 \text{ L}}{0.0500 \text{ L}}$$

(*note: volumes are in L*)

$$M_{base} = 0.118 \text{ M}$$

Compare this worked problem with Sample Exercise 4.13 and Problems 4.67 and 4.70.

Please note that these reactions noted above possess a solution stoichiometry of 1:1. For an example where the solution stoichiometry is different, see Sample Exercise 4.15 of your text. In this exercise H_2SO_4 and NaOH are used. The diprotic acid reacts with

1 mole of base. The solution to this type of titration problem requires starting out with the equation:

$$1 \, mol_{acid} = 2 \, mol_{base}$$

From this stoichiometric relationship, the equation to find the M_{acid} used in this titration can be developed just as we have seen above. Problems involving stoichiometry and similar titrations are 4.68 and 4.72-73.

Section 4
Skills for Chapter 5: Thermochemistry

Goals: to calculate heat evolved in calorimetry and heats of reaction
Skills: addition, multiplication and division

4.1 Calorimetry

Calculations in calorimetry involve measuring the change in the temperature of a chemical reaction. This is normally accomplished by noting the temperature of the reaction mixture before and after the chemical reaction has taken place. In many cases, the reaction is contained in a special measuring device called a *calorimeter*. For a reaction where mild solutions of strong acid and base are mixed together in a calorimeter, the heat evolved in the reaction is stated as:

$$q = \text{(specific heat)} \times \text{(grams of substance)} \times \Delta T$$

This expression is found on Section 5.5 of your textbook as Equation 5.19.

The mass for the mixture is determined by weighing or measuring the volume of liquid in the calorimeter and multiplying this volume by the density of the solution. The specific heat is given in a table. The ΔT is calculated from the temperature readings. The ΔT term is defined as the final temperature minus the initial temperature. A reaction where heat evolved (exothermic) will have a positive ΔT while a reaction where heat is absorbed from the environment (endothermic) will have a negative ΔT.

Let us say that when the acid and base were mixed in the calorimeter, the temperature of the solution changed from 23.5°C to 25.9°C. The final volume of the mixture was 50.0 mL. Since the density of the solution (being mostly water) is 1.00 g/mL, the aqueous solution weighs 50.0 g. The specific heat of water is stated as 4.18 J/°C-g. The ΔT is calculated as 25.9 - 23.5°C = 2.4°C. Placing these values into the above equation yields:

$$q = (4.18 \text{ J/°C-g}) \times (50.0 \text{ g}) \times (2.4°C)$$
$$q = 502 \text{ J}$$

See Sample Exercises 5.4-5.6 and Problems 5.37-5.46 of your textbook for more problems in calorimetry. Note that Problems 5.39 and 5.40 are similar to the above example.

A point to remember is that any expression that involves reactions will deal with the difference in the final state from the initial state. For any calculation using Δ (i.e. ΔT, $\Delta H°$) make a habit of thinking that $\Delta = $ (final state - initial state). Using this approach you won't get the sign of the Δ wrong.

4.2 Enthalpies of Reaction

The determination of enthalpies of reaction involves the use of the standard enthalpies of formation found in Table 5.3 and Appendix C of your textbook. The enthaply of reaction ($\Delta H°_{rxn}$) is the difference in the sums of the enthalpies of formation ($\Delta H°_f$) of the reactants and the products for a given reaction. In the calculation, we must take care to observe the sign (positive or negative) associated with the enthalpy of formation in order to obtain the correct answer. Consider the combustion of methane gas:

$$CH_4(g) + 2O_2(g) \rightarrow CO_2(g) + 2H_2O(l)$$

The calculation of $\Delta H°_{rxn}$ in kJ/mol for this reaction is:

$$\Delta H°_{rxn} = [-393.5 + 2(-285.8)] - [-74.85 + 0]$$

These values are found in Table 5.3. (*Note*: O_2 has a $\Delta H°_f$ of zero.) To begin solving, first determine the number within each set of brackets.

$$\Delta H°_{rxn} = [-965.1] - [-74.85]$$
$$\Delta H°_{rxn} = -965.1 + 74.85$$

$$\Delta H^{\circ}_{rxn} = -890.25 \text{ kJ/mol}$$

Further examples of these calculations are shown in Sample Exercise 5.9-5.10 and Problems 5.55-5.68 of your textbook. Note that Problem 5.60 involves the combustion of butane. After calculating ΔH°_{rxn}, you must find the heat produced when 1.0 g of the gas is burned. This is done by first determining the number of moles that are contained in 1.0 g of butane and then multiplying this mol quantity by ΔH°_{rxn}.

In addition to observing the sign of the ΔH°_{f}, pay close attention to the stoichiometry and the state of the products and reactants. Different states of a species (gas or liquid) will have different ΔH°_{f} values. Examine Table 5.3 of your textbook for values assigned to the different states of water.

Section 5

Skills for Chapter 6: Electronic Structure of Atoms

Goals: calculation of frequency and wavelength of photons, use of Rydberg equation
Skills: multiplication and division

5.1 Radiant Energy

In your study of radiant energy, you will investigate the relationship of the wavelength and frequency of photons. The basic equation is:

$$\nu \lambda = c$$

where ν is the frequency of the photon (expressed in Hertz) and λ is the wavelength of the photon (expressed in m). The speed of light, c, is considered a constant and is approximately 3.0×10^8 m/s. Care must be taken in this calculation to keep all values in the correct units. For instance, λ of a Na vapor lamp is 589 nm. To determine ν we can use the above equation. However, all values involving a measure of length in this calculation need to be expressed in the same units. It is most convenient to express them in meters for this problem. The wavelength is in nm, so the value would be expressed as 589×10^{-9} m, or better yet 5.89×10^{-7} m. By rearranging the above equation to solve for ν, we write:

$$\nu = \frac{c}{\lambda}$$
$$\nu = (3.00 \times 10^8 \text{ m/s}) / 5.89 \times 10^{-7} \text{m}$$
$$\nu = 5.09 \times 10^{14} \text{s}^{-1} \text{ or Hz}$$

The solution to this problem is also shown in Sample Exercise 6.1 of your text. Additional exercises on radiant energy are Problems 6.7-6.9.

This conversion of wavelength to frequency is very useful in dealing with problems in the quantum theory section where the energy of a photon is related to the frequency of the electromagnetic radiation using $E = hv$. Sample Exercise 6.2 shows this calculation for the energy of a photon emitted from a Na vapor lamp. Problems 6.13-6.14 are very similar to this example. Problems 6.15-6.22 also use this relationship.

5.2 Rydberg equation

The Rydberg equation makes use of quantum theory and relates the energy of a photon that corresponds to a transition of an electron between the orbits of a H atom. This relationship is also used to match the emission spectra of the H atoms with electronic transitions that may occur between the orbits. The equation is

$$\Delta E = R_H \left(\frac{1}{n_i^2} - \frac{1}{n_f^2} \right)$$

Since $\Delta E = hv$, the equation can be rewritten as

$$v = \frac{R_H}{h} \left(\frac{1}{n_i^2} - \frac{1}{n_f^2} \right)$$

Note that R_H and h are constants and are 2.18×10^{-18} J and 6.3×10^{-34} J-s respectively. The difficulty that is encountered in this equation is the correct calculation of the difference in the inverse squares of the n values. If $n_i = 2$ and $n_f = 4$ the calculation of the difference in the inverse square is:

$$x = \left(\frac{1}{2^2} - \frac{1}{4^2} \right)$$

$$x = \left(\frac{1}{4} - \frac{1}{16} \right) \text{ or } \left(\frac{4}{16} - \frac{1}{16} \right)$$

$$x = \frac{3}{16}$$

A common mistake that occurs in this calculation is to write the difference of the inverse squares of n is equivalent to:

$$x = \left(\frac{1}{2^2 - 4^2} \right) \quad \text{Wrong}$$

or

$$x = \left(\frac{1}{2 - 4} \right)^2 \quad \text{Wrong}$$

Both of these expressions will produce incorrect answers. You must square the n value with the $[x^2]$, invert the value with the $[1/x]$ key and then take the difference in the values.

An example of the calculation of the frequency of light emitted by a H atom when an electron falls from $n_i = 4$ to $n_f = 2$ is found in Sample Exercise 6.3 in your textbook. The Rydberg equation is also used in Problems 6.25-6.32.

5.3 Dual Nature of the Electron

Another useful relationship presented in Chapter 6 is the DeBroglie equation which relates the λ of the matter waves emitted by a particle of known mass m and traveling at a velocity v. The equation is found on Section 6.4 of your text and appears as:

$$\lambda = \frac{h}{mv}$$

Here h is Planck's constant (6.63×10^{-34} J-s). Solutions for λ or ν with this equation involve simple multiplication and division. Sample Exercise 6.4 of your text shows the use of this equation for determining λ of the matter waves of an electron.

Care must be taken when using this equation to use the correct units for m and ν. Note that 1 J $= 1$kg-m^2/s^2. All m values must be in kg and ν values in m/s. Problems 6.33-6.36 make use of this equation.

Section 6

Skills for Chapter 10: Gases

Goals: to perform calculations with gas laws, partial pressure, and effusion equations

Skills: cross multiplication, division, and roots

6.1 Gas Laws

In this section of your studies, you will be exploring relationships between pressure, P, volume, V, temperature, T, and mol quantities of gases, n. Your text will introduce you to Boyle's law, Charles's law, Avogadro's law, and the ideal gas law.

You must exercise care in two areas to avoid mistakes with these equations. The first area is temperature: all temperatures must be expressed in Kelvin, K even if the data is given to you in °C. Remember, the relationship is K = °C + 273.15. The second area is to rearrange the equation so that the left hand side only contains the term that you are seeking. All the given data would then appear on the right hand side of the equation.

Consider the use of Charles's law in finding the volume a balloon would occupy if it was heated from 25°C to 75°C. (This law is discussed in Section 10.3 of your textbook.) The volume of the balloon at 25°C is 1.00L. First, let's rework Equation 10.3 of your text for 2 sets of conditions.

$$\frac{V_1}{T_1} = \frac{V_2}{T_2}$$

From the above information we can write:

$$V_1 = 1.00 \text{ L}$$
$$T_1 = 25°\text{C, which is } 298 \text{ K}$$
$$V_2 = ?$$
$$T_2 = 75°\text{C, which is } 348 \text{ K}$$

To solve for V_2, we write:

$$\frac{V_1 T_2}{T_1} = V_2 \qquad \text{(cross multiplying } T_2)$$

$$V_2 = \frac{V_1 T_2}{T_1} \qquad \text{(switching sides)}$$

By plugging in the data, we obtain:

$$V_2 = \frac{1.00 \text{ L} \times 348 \text{ K}}{298 \text{ K}}$$

$$V_2 = 1.2 \text{ L}$$

See Problem 10.18 of your textbook for another example of Charles's law. Problem 10.17 uses Boyle's law ($PV = constant$) and Problem 10.19 uses Avogadro's law ($V = constant \times n$).

When dealing with Boyle's, Charles's, or Avogadro's law, you will often find much information in the problem. To aid you in solving the problem, follow these steps:

1) write out the gas law equation to be used.
2) sort out the given data (as set 1 or set 2).
3) rearrange the equation to solve for the unknown term.
4) enter the data and solve.

Another gas law that you will use is the ideal gas law, $PV = nRT$. It is described in Section 10.4 of your textbook. Here n is the moles of the gas and R is the gas constant (0.08206 L-atm/K-mol). This gas law will allow you to work any of the previous problems that relate the P, V, and T of a gas to the mol quantity of the gas. For instance, what volume would 1.00 g of CO_2 occupy at 1.00 atm of pressure and a temperature of 23°C? Begin this problem by writing the equation out.

$$PV = nRT$$

We were not given n in the original problem, but we can calculate it by using the equation $n = g/mw$. Here,

$$n = \frac{1.00 \text{ g}}{44.0 \text{ g} / \text{mol CO}_2}$$

and is equal to 0.0227 mol. With this information we can write:

$P = 1.00$ atm
$V = ?$
$n = 0.0227$ mol
$R = 0.08206$ L-atm/K-mol
$T = 23°C$ which must be expressed as 296 K

Rearranging the equation to solve for V, we write:

$$V = \frac{n R T}{P}$$

Plugging in the data:

$$V = \frac{(0.227 \text{ mol}) \times (0.08206 \text{ L} - \text{atm} / \text{K} - \text{mol}) \times (296 \text{ K})}{1.00 \text{ atm}}$$

$$V = 0.552 \text{ L}$$

More examples using this equation are found in Sample Exercises 10.4 and 10.5. Problems 10.23-10.33 use the ideal gas law. Problem 10.24(b) is similar to the above example.

6.2 Partial Pressures

The pressure of a gaseous mixture is dependent on the partial pressure exerted by each gas. This relationship is known as Dalton's Law of Partial Pressures and is expressed as $P_1 = X_1 P_t$, where P_1 is the pressure of gas$_1$, X_1 is the mole fraction of gas$_1$, and P_t is the total pressure of the gas. To illustrate this law, consider a container where 1.0 mol of gas$_1$ is mixed with 3.0 mols of gas$_2$. The mole fraction of gas$_1$ is calculated as follows:

$$X_1 = \frac{1.0 \text{ mol of gas}_1}{4.0 \text{mols of total gas}}$$

$$X_1 = 0.25$$

similarly,

$$X_2 = \frac{3.0 \text{ mols of gas}_2}{4.0 \text{ mols of total gas}}$$

$$X_2 = 0.75$$

IMPORTANT: The sums of all the mole fractions should always add up to 1. Since the mole fraction is a simple ratio, it has no units.

Now, to work the problem, let's assume the pressure in the container was measured to be 2.00 atm. What is the partial pressure of gas$_1$? The equation is:

$$P_1 = X_1 P_t$$

The terms to use in the equation are:

$$X_1 = 0.25 \qquad \text{(calculated above)}$$
$$P_t = 2.00 \text{ atm} \qquad \text{(given in the problem)}$$

Now by substituting into the equation we obtain,

$$P_1 = 0.25 \times 2.00 \text{ atm}$$
$$P_1 = 0.50 \text{ atm}$$

By similar reasoning we could determine that $P_2 = 1.50$ atm. Also since the gas mixture consisted of only 2 gases, if the pressure of gas$_1$

is 0.50 atm, and the total pressure of *both* gases is 2.00 atm, by difference we can find the pressure of gas$_2$ to be 1.50 atm.

Sample Exercise 10.9 makes use of the ideal gas equation to find P_1 and P_2 of 2 gases in an enclosed container. With this information, P_t can be determined. Another example is Sample Exercise 10.10 where P_1 of a gas is found and n is calculated. Other problems with this ideal gas relationship include Problems 10.35-10.46 Problems with Partial Pressures are 10.47-10.56.

6.3 Graham's Law

This law relates the effusion rate of a gas to the inverse square root of the molecular weight of the gas. The theory behind this equation is found in Section 10.8 of your textbook. You will normally use this law in comparison as:

$$\frac{r_1}{r_2} = \sqrt{\frac{M_2}{M_1}}$$

With this relationship, we must be careful with the square root sign. To demonstrate how to solve a problem with this equation let's use the following data (and for the moment forgo the units): $r_1 = 2$, $r_2 = 1$, $M_1 = ?$, and $M_2 = 100$. We must rearrange for M_1. To do so, first let us square both sides of the equation. This process will remove the square root sign. (Remember $\sqrt{x^2} = x$)

$$\left(\frac{r_1}{r_2}\right)^2 = \frac{M_2}{M_1}$$

Through cross multiplication, we can write

$$M_1 \left(\frac{r_1}{r_2}\right)^2 = M_2$$

And finally through rearrangement, the expression can be written for the unknown parameter.

$$M_1 = M_2 \left(\frac{r_2}{r_1}\right)^2$$

Using the data given in the problem.

$$r_1 = 2$$
$$r_2 = 1$$
$$M_1 = \;?$$
$$M_2 = 100$$

we substitute and write:

$$M_1 = 100 \times \left(\frac{1}{2}\right)^2$$
$$M_1 = 100 \times \left(\frac{1}{4}\right)$$
$$M_1 = 25$$

Whenever we encounter equations with square roots, we must deal with the square root and rearrange the equation before we solve for the unknown.

Another example of a calculation using Graham's law is shown in Sample Exercise 10.14 of your textbook. Problems 10.61-10.65 also uses Graham's law. Note that Problem 10.66 involves the calculation of M_2 using Graham's law.

Section 7
Skills for Chapter 13: Properties of Solutions

Goals: to determine concentrations of solutions and calculate the effect of solution strength on colligative properties

Skills: cross multiplication, division

7.1 Concentration Units

The calculations that you will perform in this chapter involve molarity, molality, normality, and mole fraction. These definitions are outlined in Section 13.4 of your text. Although they may seem similar, they involve very different units. *Molarity* involves *L* of solution, *molality* involves *kg* of solvent, and *normality* uses *equivalents* per *L* of solution. You must use the exact units specified in the definition in order to calculate the correct concentration. For instance, if you are told that 1.0 mol of solute was dissolved in 500 mL of water, you would calculate the molarity as 2.0 M (that is, 1.0 mol of solute in 0.500 L of solution, or 2.0 mol of solute in 1.000 L of solution). The use of mL instead of L would give a wrong answer. Review the Sample Exercises 13.3-13.6 and Problems 13.21-13.40 in your textbook for more examples.

7.2 Colligative Properties

There are several formulas to examine in Section 13.5. You will find:

$$P_A = X_A P^\circ_A \qquad \text{Raoult's Law}$$
$$\Delta T_b = K_b\, m \qquad \text{Boiling point elevation}$$
$$\Delta T_f = K_f m \qquad \text{Freezing point depression}$$
$$\pi = M R T \qquad \text{Osmotic Pressure}$$

Sample Exercises 13.7-13.12 demonstrate the use of these equations of colligative properties. Problems 13.41-13.60 also use these equations.

You will use the concentration units in the above section to calculate the effect of the solution strength on these colligative properties. The calculations are straightforward: the errors in the computations most often involve the use of the wrong constants (K_f vs. K_b), incorrect units (mL vs. L), or wrong concentration expression. The boiling point and freezing point equations are very similar but use different K values. For freezing point depression problems you can only use the K_f value for the solvent and not the K_b value. For osmotic pressure, the unit in the gas constant dictates the units in the equation. If 0.08206 L-atm/K-mol is used, the pressures must be in atm and the temperatures in K. Although our bodies are usually at 37°C, we must use 310 K in osmotic pressure problems relating to biochemistry.

Finally, you must remember that there is a difference in m and M. The majority of the solution calculations that you will use in this course will involve molarity, M. The molality definition, m, is used much less frequently and mainly occurs in the freezing point depression and boiling point elevation problems.

Section 8
Skills for Chapter 14: Chemical Kinetics

Goals: to calculate reaction rates, concentrations as a function of times, half-lives, and to examine the relationship of rate, temperature and activation energy

Skills: multiplication, division, logarithms, powers

8.1 Reaction Rates

The reaction rate expresses how the concentration of a product of reactant changes during the course of a reaction. The most convenient way for us to express this change is to measure the concentration as a function of time. For a simple reaction such as:

$$A \rightarrow B$$

the rate can be expressed as how the concentrations of A or B change during the time period in which the reaction is observed. If we were to plot the concentration of A as function of time, we could generate a plot, such as Figure 14.4 in your text. The average rate is calculated as the change in $[A]$ vs. the change in time:

$$\text{Average rate} = \frac{-\Delta[A]}{\Delta t}$$

The negative sign in front of $\Delta[A]$ indicates that $[A]$ is diminishing as the reaction proceeds. This makes sense, because A is the reactant. If we wished to determine the rate of this reaction as expressed by B, we would write the rate expression as $\Delta[B] / t$. Here the sign associated with B is positive; it is appearing in the reaction vessel because it is the product.

You may recognize the average rate is the slope of the line in Figure 14.4. If your calculator contains a statistical analysis package, you could enter the data ($[A]$ as y and t as $x)$ and compute the slope of the observed points. As your text mentions, some of these relationships are not linear. Just as the slope changes along the various points of Figure 14.4, so will the reaction rate. Sample Exercise 14.1 further illustrates this point.

An important point to remember in working with rate problems is the order of the reaction with respect to each reactant. Please note that the rate is experimentally determined; the stoichiometry of the reaction may have no bearing on the rate expression. For instance, after observing the reaction rates for several different concentrations of reactants, you may find that a reaction is best described by the rate law:

$$\text{Rate} = k[A]^2[B]$$

The above reaction is *second order* with respect to A and *first order* with respect to B. A change in the concentration of B with have a direct (linear) influence on the Rate. If $[A]$ is doubled, the Rate should quadruple according to the given rate expression (*e.g.* $4 = 2^2$).

If you are asked to determine the rate constant k with a given Rate, $[A]$ and $[B]$, you should first rearrange the equation and solve for k:

$$k = \frac{\text{Rate}}{[A]^2[B]}$$

If $[A] = 0.100$ M, $[B] = 0.200$ and the Rate $= 2.0 \times 10^{-5}$ M/s

$$k = \frac{2.0 \times 10^{-5} \text{ M/s}}{[0.100]^2[0.200]}$$

$$k = \frac{2.0 \times 10^{-5} \text{ M/s}}{0.00200 \text{ M}^3}$$

$$k = 0.0100 \ (\text{M}^{-2} \text{ s}^{-1})$$

Sample Exercise 14.4 is similar to this problem. For more practice, see Problems 14.14-14.24.

8.2 Concentration and Time

You will work with *first* and *second order* reactions in this portion of the chapter. Equations have been developed that relate the concentration as a function of time. The *first order* equation involves a logarithmic relationship and is best expressed as:

$$\ln\left(\frac{[A]_t}{[A]_0}\right) = -kt$$

where rate = $k[A]$

This equation is found in your text as [14.13].

In this equation k is the rate constant, t is the time at which $[A]_t$ is being determined, $[A]$ is the concentration of A at the beginning of the reaction. If you are asked to determine at what time A will fall from 1.00 M to 0.20 M with k being 0.00500/s, we would rearrange the equation and write:

$$t = \frac{-1}{k} \ln\left(\frac{[A]_t}{[A]_0}\right)$$

$$t = \frac{-1}{0.00500 \ /s} \ln\left(\frac{0.20 \ M}{1.00 \ M}\right)$$

$$t = \frac{-1}{0.00500 \ /s} \ln(0.20)$$

$$t = \frac{-1}{0.00500 \ /s} \times (-1.61)$$

$$t = 322 \ s$$

Sample Exercise 14.5 is similar to this example. Problems 14.29(b) and 14.30(b) use this equation.

A variation to this problem is to determine the concentration of A after a certain time has elapsed in the reaction. To determine this $[A]_t$, we will have to rearrange the expression and solve for $[A]_t$. But, if you look at the equation, you will notice that both $[A]$ terms are contained in the ln expression. To solve for $[A]_t$, the ln expression must be eliminated. This elimination can be legitimately done if we consider the relationship of ln and e^x. You can do this by applying the "anti-log" to the equation. This term is actually an expression for e^x. If you took the ln of a number, taking the anti-log (e^x) would restore the original number. In essence, e^x will undo what ln does. (For base$_{10}$ math, log and 10^x are similarly related.)

Therefore, to solve for $[A]_t$, we will algebraically apply e^x (the anti-log of ln) to both sides of the equation. Doing so yields:

$$\frac{[A]_t}{[A]_0} = e^{-kt} \qquad \text{(using } e^x \text{ to remove } ln\ x\text{)}$$

Now the ln term is removed. The right hand side of the equation, however, has a e^x function. Since the values of k and t are given for this type of problem, the right hand can be quickly solved.

$$[A]_t = [A]_0\, e^{-kt} \qquad \text{(through replacement)}$$

It is most important that you understand how the ln term was eliminated and A was found. Many of the problems that you will encounter in later chemistry chapters will be solved with the "log, anti-log" relationship.

To solve this problem, insert the values of $t = 100$ s, $k = 0.00500$/s and the initial concentration of 1.00 M for A_0 into the equation.

$$[A]_t = 1.00\ \text{M}\ e^{(-0.00500\ /s\ \times\ 100\ s)}$$

$$[A]_t = 1.00\ \text{M}\ e^{(-0.500)}$$

$$[A]_t = 1.00\ \text{M} \times (0.606)$$

$$[A]_t = 0.606\ \text{M} \qquad \text{(when } t = 100\ s\text{)}$$

Use this approach to solve the concentrations of first order decay reactions for Problems 14.29(a) and 14.30(a).

A common mistake made in working these problems is assuming:

$$\ln\left(\frac{[A]_t}{[A]_0}\right) = \frac{\ln [A]_t}{\ln [A]_0} \qquad \textit{Wrong !}$$

This assumption is incorrect. The *ln* term cannot be distributed to the numerator and the denominator. The quotient of the expression must first be found and then *ln* applied to the result. You must use "anti-logs" properly to solve for this type of problem.

Another formula that you may see for *first order* reactions is the expression for half-life. This expression relates the time for a product to decay to half of its original concentration. The derivation of this relationship is not essential to know, but the formula is. The half-life, $t_{1/2}$ is expressed as:

$$t_{1/2} = \frac{0.693}{k}$$

where k is the rate constant for the *first order* reaction. This equation is found in your textbook as [14.15]. The solution for either $t_{1/2}$ or k is found by cross multiplication. Sample Exercise 14.6 demonstrates the use of this equation. Problems 14.27, 14.28, and 14.29(c) are similar to this exercise.

The *second order* reaction relationship of concentration and time is best expressed as:

$$\frac{1}{[A]_t} = kt + \frac{1}{[A]_0}$$

where rate $= k[A]^2$. This equation appears in Chapter 14 of your textbook as [14.16]. It is derived using calculus and is discussed in Section 14.3 of your textbook. You are not required to perform the derivation with these problems, but you must remember the form of the equation. It is quite different from the *first order* equation.

If you are asked to determine the concentration of A at some time t, simply plug in the data and solve. Remember to use the $[1/x]$ after solving the right hand side of the equation.

Other types of problems will involve determining at what time t the concentration of A will decrease from the original value to some lower level. If you are given $[A]_t$, $[A]_0$ and k, the equation can be rearranged to find t as:

$$t = \frac{1}{k} \times \left(\frac{1}{[A]_t} - \frac{1}{[A]_0} \right)$$

Pitfalls in these calculations are the assumption that the concentration data in the brackets can be written as:

$$\frac{1}{[A]_t - [A]_0} \qquad \textit{Wrong!}$$

You must start solving the equation from within the brackets. Use the $[1/x]$ key to calculate the reciprocal of each concentration and then subtract them.

The half-life equation for a *second order* reaction is expressed as:

$$t_{1/2} = \frac{1}{k[A]_0}$$

and is found in your textbook as [14.17].

Note that the *second order* half-life equation is dependent on the rate constant, while the *first order* equation is independent of k. This information can be most helpful when you are asked to determine the order of a reaction when given only $[A]$ and t data (see Sample Exercise 14.7 of your textbook).

8.3 Activation Energies

One of the larger equations that you will deal with in general chemistry relates the rate constants, temperature, and activation energy. It is expressed as:

$$\ln\left(\frac{k_1}{k_2}\right) = \frac{E_a}{R}\left(\frac{1}{T_2} - \frac{1}{T_1}\right)$$

and is found in your textbook as [14.22]. A problem using this equation to solve for the k value of a given reaction at a higher temperature is demonstrated in Sample Exercise 14.8 of your text. Problems 14.39-14.48, 14.51 and 14.52 reinforce this concept.

There are several important points to keep in mind when you are working problems with these equations.

- Express the temperature in K.
- Use the gas constant 8.314 J/K-mol.
- Use the "anti-logs" to help solve for the k value in the ln expression (see Section 8.2 of this booklet).
- Take the reciprocals of the temperatures before you subtract them.

Section 9

Skills for Chapter 15: Chemical Equilibrium

Goals: to calculate concentrations of products and reactants at equilibrium, and equilibrium constants

Skills: cross multiplication, powers, and roots

9.1 Calculations with Equilibrium Expressions

Using LeChâtelier's principle, the equilibrium expression for the chemical equation $A + B \rightarrow 2C$ is written as:

$$K_c = \frac{[C]^2}{[A][B]}$$

If you are given the equilibrium concentrations of A, B, and C, the equilibrium constant can be determined by entering these concentrations into the equation. For instance, if $[A] = 0.10$ M $[B] = 0.20$ M and $[C] = 0.50$ M, we can write:

$$K_c = \frac{[0.50]^2}{[0.10][0.20]}$$

and

$$K_c = 13$$

Sample Exercise 15.7 show the calculation of K_c for the Haber process. Other problems concerning the calculation of K_c are Problems 15.19-15.26.

A variation to this problem may involve the determination of [C] if [A], [B], and K_c is given to you. If $K_c = 13$ with $[A] = 0.50$ M and $[B] = 0.25$, let us arrange the above equation to solve for [C].

$$K_c = \frac{[C]^2}{[0.50][0.25]}$$

Next, each side of the equation is multiplied by the denominator, [0.50][0.25]. This act leaves only the term $[C]^2$ on the right hand side of the equation.

$$13 \times (\ [0.50][0.25]\ ) = [C]^2$$

where, by rearranging and multiplying the numbers we generate,

$$\sqrt{[C]^2} = \sqrt{1.6}$$

$$[C] = 1.3$$

The equilibrium concentration of C is 1.3 M.

There may be times in solving the equilibrium problems where the determination of a concentration involves taking the third or fourth root of the expression. For instance, let's look at the production of ammonia from nitrogen and hydrogen (the Haber process, as described in Section 15.4 of your text).

$$2N_2{}_{(g)} + 3H_2{}_{(g)} \leftrightarrow 2NH_3{}_{(g)}$$

The equilibrium expression for this reaction is:

$$K_c = \frac{[NH_3]^2}{[N_2]^2[H_2]^3}$$

To solve for K_c, we must raise the equilibrium concentration to the power of 3 for hydrogen, while squaring the other concentrations. You will need to use the powers function of y^x on your calculator (see Section 1 of this workbook).

If, instead, you wish to solve for the hydrogen concentration using a given K_c value and known equilibrium concentration of ammonia and nitrogen, the equation must be rearranged.

$$[H_2]^3 = \frac{[NH_3]^2}{K_c\ [N_2]^2}$$

$$[H_2]^3 = \frac{[NH_3]^2}{K_c\,[N_2]^2}$$

If $K_c = 0.105$, $[NH_3] = 0.030$ M, and $[N_2] = 0.050$, what is $[H_2]$? Plugging in the numbers, we can write:

$$[H_2]^3 = \frac{(0.030)^2}{(0.105)\,(0.050)^2}$$

$$[H_2]^3 = 3.43$$

$$[H_2] = (3.43)^{1/3}$$

$$[H_2] = 1.5 \quad \text{(using the $[y^x]$ function)}$$

In order to work any of these types of problems, it is most important that you be able to write the correct equilibrium constant expression for the reaction. If you are in doubt as how to construct the expression, look back at Section 15.2 of your textbook and Sample Exercises 15.1 - 15.3 concerning the effects of stoichiometry and the states of the products and reactants (homogeneous or heterogeneous reaction) on the equilibrium expression.

9.2 Calculations of Equilibrium Concentrations

A second use of the equilibrium expression involves the determination of the concentrations of the products and the reactants at equilibrium. If the stoichiometry of the reaction is known (allowing the equilibrium expression to be written) and K_c is known, then the equilibrium concentrations may be found.

However, the solution to this problem is not always straightforward. In most cases, we only know the initial concentrations of the products and the reactants; we don't know the equilibrium concentrations. To calculate these equilibrium concentrations we must figure out how much the initial concentrations of products and reactants change, based upon the relationship defined by the equilibrium expression.

To help explain how such a solution to this problem is found, we will introduce here the "equilibrium checkbook". This teaching tool will allow us to quickly determine the concentrations of all equilibrium products and reactants. The checkbook concept is patterned very much like the checkbook that you are maintaining with a bank in your town. Just as keeping a good record of all deposits and drafts to the account enables you to balance the account, the equilibrium concentration of products and reactants can be readily determined with this tool.

To see how the checkbook works, let's return to the "alphabet" reaction of Section 9.1 of this booklet: A + B → 2C. This balanced equation shows that 2 moles of product C are produced when 1 mole of A reacts with 1 mole of B. The equilibrium expression is then written as

$$K_C = \frac{[C]^2}{[A][B]}$$

For the purpose of this example, let us say that $K_C = 0.0100$. The initial concentrations of both A and B are 0.500 M. The initial concentration of C is zero.

Because there is no C present, we can easily see that the reaction will proceed toward the right; that is, some C will be produced. However, there are times when you will be asked to perform calculations such as these when the concentration of the "products" (those written on the right-hand side of the equation) are not zero. To determine which direction a reaction will take (e.g. to the right or to the left), you should calculate the reaction quotient, Q (this is discussed in Section 15.5 of your text). The formula seems identical to the equilibrium expression, but note that the initial concentrations, as noted by ( ) brackets, of the products and reactants are used rather than the equilibrium concentrations, as noted by [ ] brackets.

$$Q = \frac{(C)^2}{(A)(B)}$$

By comparing Q to K_C, the pathway can be determined. Sample Exercise 15.9 specifically addresses this calculation.

In the sample problem for demonstrating the equilibrium checkbook, we have the task of finding [C] from the equilibrium equation. The setup of the checkbook is shown below:

Species	A	B	2C
initial			
Δ			
equilibrium			

In the top row (labeled species), the reactants and products of the chemical equation are written. The stoichiometry of the equations is also entered in the top row of each column. Note that the double line separates the reactants and products and serves in place of the ↔ symbol. The other rows are labeled: initial, Δ (for change), and equilibrium. These entries will pertain to how the concentration of each reactant and product change during the course of the reaction.

With the given information, we can set up the entries in the equilibrium checkbook. Our initial concentrations are entered in the initial row under the proper column of each reactant and product.

Species	A	B	2C
initial	0.500 M	0.500 M	0 M
Δ			
equilibrium			

The next stage is to determine the changes (withdrawals and deposits) to each account. From the stoichiometry of the reaction, every 1 mol of A and 1 mol of B that react produce 2 mols of C. With this reasoning, if x mol of A and x mol of B react, then 2x mols of C are produced. Since A and B are reactants, their concentrations should be depleted as the reaction proceeds. This "withdrawal" can be entered in the checkbook in the Δ row as -x. Similarly, the "deposits" of +2x to the C column can be entered, as shown below:

Species	A	B	2C
initial	0.500 M	0.500 M	0 M
Δ	-x	-x	+2x
equilibrium			

The last step is to add up the activity in each account. This "bottom line" is the equilibrium concentration as a function of initial concentrations and x. By adding the initial and Δ entries together for each product and reactant we find:

Species	A	B	2C
initial	0.500 M	0.500 M	0 M
Δ	-x	-x	+2x
equilibrium	0.500 M - x	0.500 M - x	2x

The entries in the bottom row are the equilibrium concentrations as a function of the initial concentration and x. Since we want to know the equilibrium concentrations as a simple number rather than in terms of initial concentrations and x, we must solve for the value of x. Once we know x, we can directly express [A], [B], and [C].

The solution of x lies in the use of the equilibrium expression. By substituting these data into the equilibrium expression, we can write:

$$0.0100 = \frac{[2x]^2}{[0.500 - x][0.500 - x]}$$

Note that we have one equation and one unknown. To solve for x, we must employ our algebraic skills. For this problem, the solution lies in noting that the equation can be simplified to:

$$0.0100 = \frac{[2x]^2}{[0.500 - x]^2}$$

If we now take the square root of both sides, the x^2 term can be reduced to x, thereby making the equation much easier to solve.

$$\sqrt{0.0100} = \sqrt{\frac{[2x]^2}{[0.500-x]^2}}$$

which simplifies to

$$0.0100 = \frac{[2x]}{[0.500-x]}$$

By cross multiplication and rearrangement, the following equations show the solution for x:

$$0.100 \times [0.500 - x] = [2x]$$

$$0.0500 - 0.100x = 2x$$

$$0.0500 = 2.100x$$

$$x = \frac{0.0500}{2.100}$$

$$x = 0.024$$

Having found x, the equilibrium values of A, B, and C can be calculated.

$$[A] = (0.500 - 0.024) = 0.476 \text{ mol/L remaining of A}$$

$$[B] = (0.500 - 0.024) = 0.476 \text{ mol/L remaining of B}$$

$$[C] = (2 \times 0.024) = 0.048 \text{ mol/L produced of C}$$

These values are the equilibrium concentrations of the reactants and products.

The use of the checkbook will allow you to setup and solve every equilibrium problem that is discussed in your text. Not all problems will be solved by the same exact algebraic methods shown above, but the solutions are similar.

You should also examine Sample Exercise 15.11 in your text and note the similarity in the checkbook to the above problem. The difference in this example is that the concentrations of the reactants are not the same, hence solution is not obtained by taking the square root of both sides of the equation. Instead, the quadratic formula is used to find the value of x. The following Practice Exercise deals with a cylinder filled with only "reactants" and the concentrations of the products (x) are calculated. Try applying this method to the other Sample Problems 15.31-15.42

The checkbook method can be a powerful tool in calculating equilibrium concentrations. This method can be applied to problems in Chapters 15 - 18 of you text. The correct use of this equation requires that you must have a balanced equation and an equilibrium expression.

Section 10
Skills for Chapter 16: Acid-Base Equilibria

Goals: to calculate pH values, K_a values, and equilibrium concentration of products and reactants of acid-base reactions

Skills: multiplication, division, logarithms, powers, roots, and quadratic equations

In this section on aqueous equilibrium, you will be studying methods to calculate the equilibrium concentrations of products and reactants of a chemical reaction. Of the many forms of aqueous equilibrium that exist, acid-base equilibria will be the first in your studies. They are presented first because they can be easily studied in your laboratory section. The basic concepts that you learn in this chapter can be directly applied to the many forms of equilibria that you will encounter in upper level chemistry courses.

10.1 pH Calculations

When HCl is added to H_2O, the following reaction occurs:

$$HCl\textit{(aq)} \leftrightarrow H^+\textit{(aq)} + Cl^-\textit{(aq)}$$

The value of $[H^+]$ can vary significantly. As your text mentions, the range of these values is controlled by the solvent. Water is capable of producing $[H^+]$,

$$H_2O\textit{(aq)} \leftrightarrow H^+\textit{(aq)} + OH^-\textit{(aq)} \qquad K_a = 1.0 \times 10^{-14}$$

Water will normally have a concentration of H^+ of 1×10^{-7} M. If a strong acid such as HCl is added to the water, the $[H^+]$ will increase.

Instead of always trying to remember the hydrogen ion concentration of an acid solution as a value expressed to a power, chemists have simplified the values through the concept of pH. By definition:

$$pH = -\log[H^+]$$

If you know the H^+ equilibrium concentration, the pH may be solved by entering the value of $[H^+]$ into your calculator, pressing the [*log*] key, and then the [+/-] to make the value positive. For example, if the $[H^+]$ is found to be 3.0×10^{-5} M, then the pH is calculated as:

$$pH = -\log[3.0 \times 10^{-5}]$$
$$pH = -(-4.52)$$
$$pH = 4.52$$

Please note that there are two types of logarithmic functions on your calculator, [*log*] and [*ln*]. The pH definition is based on *log* and not *ln*.

We can check the pH calculations with a given $[H^+]$ by using the log relationship of powers to pH.

$$[H^+] = 1.0 \times 10^{-3}$$
$$pH = -\log[1.0 \times 10^{-3}]$$
$$pH = -(-3.00)$$
$$pH = 3.00$$

By similar reasoning, if $[H^+] = 1.0 \times 10^{-5}$, then the pH = 5.00. For the first example worked in this section where $[H^+] = 3.0 \times 10^{-5}$ M, we can predict that the pH should lie between 4 and 5. This second check with our "cerebral calculator" can be of aid in confirming the answer from our pocket calculator. A similar example is demonstrated in Sample Exercises 16.6 of your textbook. Also, see Problems 16.23-16.27.

Another calculation that will be used in these studies will be the determination of the $[H^+]$ if we are given the pH. This calculation can be performed by using the concept of anti-logs. From our earlier definition,

$$pH = -\log[H^+]$$

$$-pH = \log[H^+] \qquad (\text{multiplying both sides by} -1)$$

$$10^{-pH} = 10^{\log[H^+]} \qquad (\text{using the anti-log relationship})$$

$$10^{-pH} = [H^+]$$

$$[H^+] = 10^{-pH}$$

To perform these calculations, use the $[y^x]$ or the $[10^x]$ as you did in the previous chapter. If the pH is 5.50 then,

$$[H^+] = 10^{-5.50}$$
$$[H^+] = 3.2 \times 10^{-6} \, M$$

A similar example is shown in Sample Exercise 16.7 of your textbook. Problems 16.25 and 16.26 reinforce this concept. Note that both involve the concept of pOH. The relationship between pH and pOH is discussed in Section 16.4 of your textbook.

You will need to determine whether or not the acid (or base) involved in the reaction is a strong or weak species. As mentioned in your text, the $[H^+]$ for strong acids is usually the initial concentration of the reactants (*i.e.* HCl) because of complete dissociation, whereas the $[H^+]$ for weak acids is determined from the equilibrium expression. For practice with strong acids, look at Sample Exercises 16.8 and Problems 16.29, 16.31 and 16.32. Examples using strong bases are Sample Exercise 16.9 and Problems 16.30 and 16.33-16.36.

10.2 Equilibrium Calculations

When dealing with weak acids or bases, it is necessary to use the equilibrium expression to calculate the $[H^+]$. To determine this value, we will introduce the concept of an "equilibrium checkbook". This teaching tool will allow us to quickly determine the concentrations of all equilibrium products and reactants. The checkbook aids in the determination of the equilibrium concentration of products, [H⁺], and reactants.

To start, let's consider how the pH of a 0.10M solution of acetic acid is determined. The balanced stoichiometric equation is listed below:

$$HC_2H_3O_2(aq) \leftrightarrow H^+(aq) + C_2H_3O_2^-(aq)$$

to make our writing a bit more simple, let OAc⁻ = $C_2H_3O_2^-$. Also, the term *(aq)* will be dropped for this homogenous reaction.

$$HOAc \leftrightarrow H^+ + OAc^-$$

The equilibrium expression is written as,

$$K_a = \frac{[H^+][OAc^-]}{[HOAc]}$$

We have the task of finding [H⁺] from this equation. All we know is that the initial concentration of HOAc, (HOAc) = 0.10 M and the $K_a = 1.8 \times 10^{-5}$ (from Table 16.2 of your textbook). This information is enough to set up the equilibrium checkbook. We see from the acid dissociation equation that the H⁺ and OAc⁻ must come from the dissociation of HOAc. (Please note that here the assumption is made that the contribution of H⁺ from the auto dissociation of water is negligible as compared to that of the acid.)

Any products that are formed, H⁺ and OAc⁻, must occur from a "withdrawal" from our chemical account that holds the initial "deposit" of the weak acid, HOAc. Also, note that the use of [ ] denotes the equilibrium concentration, while ( ) is used for the initial concentration.

The setup of the check is shown below:

Species	HOAc	H⁺	OAc⁻
initial	0.10 M	0 M	0 M
Δ			
equilibrium			

The next stage is to determine the changes (withdrawals and deposits) to each account. From the stoichiometry, for each mole of HOAc that undergoes dissociation (withdrawal), one mole of H^+ and one mole of OAc^- is generated (deposits). If x moles of H^+ and x moles of OAc^- are produced, they must have originated from x moles of HOAc (based upon the stoichiometry of the problem). Now that these relationships have been determined, the second row (change) of the checkbook may be entered.

Species	HOAc	H^+	OAc^-
initial	0.10 M	0 M	0 M
Δ	$-x$	$+x$	$+x$
equilibrium			

The last step is to add up the activity in each account. This "bottom line" is the equilibrium concentration as a function of initial concentrations and x.

Species	HOAc	H^+	OAc^-
initial	0.10 M	0 M	0 M
Δ	$-x$	$+x$	$+x$
equilibrium	0.10 M - x	x	x

To solve for $[H^+]$, we substitute each of the final concentration equations back into the equilibrium expression.

$$K_a = \frac{[x][x]}{[0.10 - x]}$$

Please note that the contribution of $[H^+]$ from the autodissociation of H_2O is negligible when dealing with weak acid solutions. Here $[H^+]$ = $[OAc^-]$ because they both came from the dissociation of HOAc. Therefore, the numerator is expressed as x^2. Also, since $K_a = 1.8 \times 10^{-5}$, the equation reduces to:

$$1.8 \times 10^{-5} = \frac{[x]^2}{[0.10 - x]}$$

Now, we have one equation with one unknown. There are two methods for the determination of x. The first involves the use of the quadratic equation (found in Appendix A.of your textbook). By cross multiplying and grouping like terms we can write:

$$x^2 + 1.8 \times 10^{-5}x - 1.8 \times 10^{-6} = 0$$

Using the quadratic formula, let $a = 1$, $b = 1.8 \times 10^{-5}$, and $c = -1.8 \times 10^{-6}$. By plugging these values into the equation, we find x to be 1.3×10^{-3} or -1.35×10^{-3}. Since we cannot have negative values for concentrations, we accept only the first answer.

Let's take a moment to see what we have found: $x = [H^+]$ and $[OAc^-]$, $[HOAc] = 0.10 - 1.3 \times 10^{-3} = 0.0987$ M (but best expressed as 0.10 M using the correct number of significant figures). Note that this change, x, is only 1.3% of the original value. The calculation, which is referred to as the % ionization is as follows:

$$\text{\% ionized} = \frac{[x]}{(HOAc)} \times 100\%$$

Because the change of x in [HOAc] is not significant, we may solve this dissociation equation in a more direct fashion by eliminating x from the denominator.

$$1.8 \times 10^{-5} = \frac{[x]^2}{[0.10 - x]}$$

$$x^2 = 1.8 \times 10^{-6}$$

$$x = 1.3 \times 10^{-3}$$

Care must be taken in the removal of x from the denominator. This removal (which is an approximation to the solution) can only be done if the change in reactant is found to be insignificant. For your studies in acid base equilibrium, this level of insignificance is said to occur when $x < 5\%$ of the original concentration. If you find $x < 5\%$ of the original reactant concentration you may use the shortcut. If $x > 5\%$ you must use the quadratic equation to correctly solve for x. (Of course, you may use the quadratic equation in all of these problems to find x.)   However, since the K_a values of the acids you use in your calculations are very small, and you will rarely work with acids much less than 0.001 M in these calculations, you will probably be able to use the shortcut for most of your calculations.

From the definition of equilibrium concentration of the products and reactants, it can be determined that $[H^+]$ and $[OAc^-] = 1.3 \times 10^{-3}$ M and $[HOAc] = 0.10$ M. The pH of the equation is $-\log[x]$ and is calculated as 2.89.

Sample Exercises 16.10-16.12 in your textbook involve calculations with the K_a expression. Sample Exercise 16.13 introduces you to polyprotic acids (acids with more than one H^+ and K_a), while Exercises 16.14 - 16.15 present the calculation of the pOH using the initial concentrations of the weak base and K_b. Note the similarity in the solutions using pOH with K_b to that of pH and K_a. Use the equilibrium checkbook to set up the problems and find the solutions.

Additional problems othat can be solved with this approach are 16.39-16.58 for weak acids and 16.59-16.66 for weak bases. When given the % ionization, as with Problem 16.43 you can quickly find x and enter this value directly into the checkbook for the determination of the equilibrium concentrations of products and reactants.

Section 11
Skills for Chapter 17: Aspects of Equilibria

Goals: to calculate equilibrium concentrations of products and reactants in common ion problems, to calculate the pH of buffer solution, to calculate solubility and K_{sp}

Skills: multiplication, division, logarithms, powers, roots and quadratic equations

In the previous section you were introduced to acid-base equilibria. In this section of your text, you will further explore these concepts by studying the effect of common ions on equilibrium, buffer solutions, and solubility equilibria.

11.1 Common Ion Effect

In the previous section we studied the equilibrium reaction where acetic acid (HOAc), a weak acid, undergoes dissociation to form:

$$HOAc \leftrightarrow H^+ + OAc^-$$

If we know the initial concentration of HOAc and the K_a value, we can determine the equilibrium concentrations of H^+ and OAc^-. So far, these problems have only dealt with adding HOAc to pure water (the initial concentrations of the products have been 0). Consider how the reaction would be affected if both HOAc and OAc^-, in the form of sodium acetate (NaOAc), were added to the solution. NaOAc is a strong electrolyte and undergoes complete dissociation. Based on LeChâtelier's principle,

$$K_a = \frac{[H^+][OAc^-]}{[HOAc]} \qquad \text{where } K_a = 1.8 \times 10^{-5}$$

the amount of H^+ that is produced is limited by the presence of OAc^- in the reaction vessel. If the initial amount of HOAc is 0.30 M and the initial amount of NaOAc is 0.10 M, we can set up the checkbook to find the $[H^+]$.

Species	HOAc	H^+	OAc⁻
initial	0.30 M	0 M	0.10 M
Δ			
equilibrium			

The next step in solving the problem is to write in the activity in this account. From the stoichiometry of this reaction, for every mole of HOAc that undergoes dissociation, a mole of H^+ and a mole of OAc⁻ is produced. This activity is described as:

Species	HOAc	H^+	OAc⁻
initial	0.30 M	0 M	0.10 M
Δ	-x	+x	+x
equilibrium			

Balancing the checkbook yields:

Species	HOAc	H^+	OAc⁻
initial	0.30 M	0 M	0.10 M
Δ	-x	+x	+x
equilibrium	0.30 M - x	x	0.10 M + x

Substituting the equilibrium concentrations from the checkbook and the value of K_a allows us to write the expression:

$$1.8 \times 10^{-5} = \frac{[x][0.10 + x]}{[0.30 - x]}$$

To find the $[H^+]$, the equation must be solved for x. If we began to multiply and group like terms, we would have to use the quadratic formula to reach the solution. However, it is possible to make certain assumptions for this reaction that will permit a good approximation of x to be found. In the above equation note that x is in the numerator and denominator. If this change in the equilibrium concentration from x is insignificant, the expression reduces to:

$$1.8 \times 10^{-5} = \frac{[x](0.10)}{(0.30)}$$

This shortcut can only be used if $x < 5\%$ of the initial reactant concentration. (See Section 10.2 of this workbook for an explanation.) If we rearrange to solve for x, we can write:

$$(1.8 \times 10^{-5})(0.30) = x(0.10)$$

$$x = \frac{(1.8 \times 10^{-5})(0.30)}{(0.10)}$$

$$x = 5.4 \times 10^{-5}$$

This value x is the $[H^+]$. Note that the change of x does not alter significantly the concentration of HOAc and OAc$^-$.

For this approximation to be used in the solution of x, it is most important that the value x not be $> 5\%$ of the initial concentration. (This calculation is done in the preceding section of this booklet.) If $x > 5\%$, then the quadratic equation must be used to correctly solve the equation.

As you work with these problems, you will begin to understand when the approximation is valid to use. If your K_a is very small ($< 1 \times 10^{-4}$), and the initial concentrations of reactants and products are large (0.10 to 1 M), you will probably use the approximation. Make it a habit to confirm that $x < 5\%$.

Other examples of the effect of common ions on weak acids can be found in Sample Exercise 17.1 and 17.2 of your textbook. Also, see Problems 17.5-17.8.

11.2 Buffers

In the above example, the [H⁺] produced from the weak acid dissociation is shown to be controlled by the initial concentrations of reactant and products and the equilibrium constant. In Chapter 17 of your text, an equation is described that relates the pH (equilibrium H⁺) to the concentration of the conjugate acid-base pairs. It is called the Henderson-Hasselbalch equation and is written as:

$$pH = pK_a + \log\left(\frac{base}{acid}\right)$$

and is found in [17.9] in Section 17.2 of your textbook.

More commonly, this expression is known as the buffer equation. By adjusting the (base)/(acid) ratio of a conjugate acid-base pair, the pH can be controlled. Using this equation, go back to the previous problem and solve for the pH of the mixture. From the given data (OAc⁻) = 0.10M and (HOAc) = 0.30 M. To find the pK_a value we take the negative log of K_a.

$$pK_a = -\log K_a$$
$$pK_a = -\log (1.8 \times 10^{-5})$$
$$pK_a = -(-4.74)$$
$$pK_a = 4.74$$

To solve for the pH, enter the data into the buffer equation.

$$pH = 4.74 + \log\left(\frac{(0.10)}{(0.30)}\right)$$

$$pH = 4.74 + (-0.48)$$
$$pH = 4.26$$

Sample Exercises 17.3 in your textbook is very similar to this problem. A checkbook approach is used to find [H⁺]. Problems 17.12 and 17.13 can also be solved with this approach. Also see Problems 17.14-17.16 and 17.20.

An important use of this equation is to calculate the ratio of (base)/(acid) required to make a specific pH. Let's say you wished to make a buffer solution where the pH = 4.50. If you were using the HOAc and NaOAc conjugate pair to make the buffer solution, in what ratio would you mix them? We can rearrange the buffer equation to solve for the ratio.

$$pH = pK_a + \log\left(\frac{base}{acid}\right)$$

$$\log\left(\frac{base}{acid}\right) = pH - pK_a$$

$$\left(\frac{base}{acid}\right) = 10^{(pH - pK_a)}$$

Entering the data into this equation, we can write:

$$\left(\frac{base}{acid}\right) = 10^{(4.50 - 4.74)}$$

$$\left(\frac{base}{acid}\right) = 10^{(-0.24)}$$

$$\left(\frac{base}{acid}\right) = 0.58$$

The base to acid ratio should be 0.58 to achieve a pH of 4.50. If you wished to use a (HOAc) of 0.10 M, the (OAc⁻) would need to be 0.058 M. Use this approach to solve Problem 17.19. *HINT:* Remember that log (1) = 0. If the base to acid ratio is 1, the pK_a of the acid-base pair is the pH.

In Section 17.2 of your textbook, you are introduced to the calculation of the pH of a buffered solution when a strong acid or base is added to the buffer solution. To solve a problem like this, we will first have to use the checkbook and then the buffer equation. For this example, let's look at the effect of adding 0.02 M HCl to a buffered solution containing 0.10 M HOAc and 0.10 M NaOAc. (Since the (base)/(acid) = 1, the pH before the HCl is added to the solution is the pK_a value of 4.74.) The checkbook for the balanced equation is started as:

Species	HOAc	H^+	OAc^-
initial	0.10 M	0.02 M	0.10 M
Δ			
equilibrium			

Note that the $[H^+]$ is not 0 here, but the concentration of the strong acid that is added to the buffer solution. This addition should force the reaction to the left; that is, excess H^+ will react with OAc^- to produce HOAc. Filling out the change columns yields:

Species	HOAc	H^+	OAc^-
initial	0.10 M	0.02 M	0.10 M
Δ	$+x$	$-x$	$-x$
equilibrium			

Completing the checkbook, we can write,

Species	HOAc	H^+	OAc^-
initial	0.10 M	0.02 M	0.10 M
Δ	$+x$	$-x$	$-x$
equilibrium	$0.10\ M + x$	$0.02\ M - x$	$0.10\ M - x$

A driving force in this aqueous buffer chemistry problem is the strong acid which is added to the solution reacts completely with the OAc^- to form HOAc. If 0.02 of strong acid is added to the solution (1.0L total volume of solution), then the x term in the above equation is 0.02. The H^+ concentration will be 0 after the reaction is over. (Note: an assumption in your text is that H^+ is describing the strong acid concentration. After the reaction is over, the strong acid should be "neutralized" and its concentration 0. This does not mean that there are 0 H^+ in the solution. The HOAc will provide a small amount as well as the solvent, water. But for our purpose of buffer calculations, the concentration is 0.)

From the final row of the checkbook, it can be determined that [HOAc] = 0.12 M and [OAc⁻] = 0.08 M. If we place these numbers into the buffer equation, we can calculate the pH.

$$pH = 4.74 + \log\left(\frac{0.08}{0.12}\right)$$

$$pH = 4.74 + \log(0.67)$$

$$pH = 4.74 + (-0.18)$$

$$pH = 4.56$$

HINT: It is a good practice to check the logic of the calculation. If you add an acid to a buffer solution, the pH should decrease from the original value. If you add a base to a buffer solution, the pH should increase. If the opposite, you have probably reversed the concentrations of the base/acid ratio.

Sample Exercise 17.5 can be solved with the approach. Note, however, a strong base is added to the buffer instead of an acid (as above) with this approach. Also, try Problems 17.17 and 17.18.

This approach to buffers is also useful when titrating a weak acid with a strong base (*e.g.* titrating HOAc with NaOH). At the start of the titration, the only OAc⁻ present is from the weak acid dissociation. When the strong base is added to the solution the following reaction occurs:

$$HOAc + OH^- \rightarrow OAc^- + H_2O$$

This reaction proceeds toward completion; that is, for every 1 mol of OH⁻ that is introduced into the HOAc solution, 1 mol of HOAc is consumed and 1 mol of OAc⁻ is produced. Since OH is added in significant quantities, the [OAc⁻] is primarily the result of the titration. The amount of OAc⁻ (*x*) from the weak acid dissociation is negligible when compared to the amount produced by the titration reaction. Hence, the titration produces the buffer solution. The pH of this solution is found using the buffer equation.

The solution of pH requires us to find the [HOAc] and [OAc⁻] resulting from the titration. Consider a 50.0 mL solution of 0.100 M HOAc to which 25.0 mL of a 0.0700 M standardized base solution of NaOH has been added. The original mol amount of HOAc is 0.100 M × 0.0500 L = 0.00500 mol. The mol amount of OH⁻ that has been added to the solution is (0.0700 M × 0.0250 L) = 0.00175 mol. The mol amount of HOAc remaining is (0.00500 - 0.00175) = 0.00325 mol. The mol amount of OAc⁻ produced is 0.00175 mol.

To use the buffer equation we must express OAc- and HOAC in terms of concentration. This requires us to express each in terms of molarity. To do this, we must first calculate the total volume of the solution: (50.0 mL of acid + 25.0 mL of base) = 75.0 mL, or 0.075 L. Next, introduce these data into the buffer equation.

$$pH = pK_a + \log\left(\frac{\frac{0.00175 \text{ mol OAc}^-}{0.075 \text{ L}}}{\frac{0.00325 \text{ mol of HOAc}}{0.075 \text{ L}}}\right)$$

$$pH = pK_a + \log(0.538)$$

$$pH = 4.74 + (-0.269) \quad \text{since } pK_a = 4.74$$

$$pH = 4.47$$

See Sample Exercise for a similar problem. Also apply this problem solving methodology to Problems 17.27-17.32.

11.3 Solubility

Another form of equilibria is solubility. Consider the process of dissolving AgCl in water.

$$AgCl_{(s)} \leftrightarrow Ag^+{}_{(aq)} + Cl^-{}_{(aq)} \qquad K_{sp} = 1.8 \times 10^{-10}$$

Since this is a heterogeneous reaction, the equilibrium expression is written as:

$$K_{sp} = [Ag^+][Cl^-]$$

The AgCl is a solid and will not enter into the equilibrium calculation or the checkbook.

The K_{sp} expression is useful in determining the molar solubility of a compound. If excess AgCl is placed in water, the K_{sp} expression will define the maximum allowable product of two species. We can see how this works if we set up the checkbook.

Species	Ag^+	Cl^-
initial	0 M	0 M
Δ		
equilibrium		

Because $AgCl_{(s)}$ is not part of the heterogeneous equilibrium expression, it is not listed here. (Remember, the concentration of a solid cannot change, therefore only the soluble species in this reaction are listed.)

The change column is determined from the stoichiometry of the equation. Here 1 mole of $AgCl_{(s)}$ yields 1 mole of $Ag^+_{(aq)}$ and 1 mole of $Cl^-_{(aq)}$. If x moles of AgCl dissolve, then the checkbook becomes:

Species	Ag^+	Cl^-
initial	0 M	0 M
Δ	$+x$	$+x$
equilibrium		

The equilibrium concentrations are calculated as:

Species	Ag^+	Cl^-
initial	0 M	0 M
Δ	$+x$	$+x$
equilibrium	$+x$	$+x$

If we substitute these values for the equilibrium concentrations into the equilibrium equation, we obtain:

$$K_{sp} = [x][x] \qquad \text{or}$$

$$K_{sp} = [x]^2$$

$$x = \sqrt{K_{sp}}$$

Solving for x will tell us the molar concentrations of each ion in solution as well as the molar amount of solid that was dissolved. Plugging in K_{sp} and solving this expression yields:

$$x = \sqrt{1.8 \times 10^{-10}}$$

$$x = 1.4 \times 10^{-5}$$

The molar solubility of $AgCl_{(s)}$ is 1.4×10^{-5} M.

The stoichiometry of the equation plays an important part in determining the molar solubility of a compound. Consider the salt, CaF_2. The balance dissociation equation and equilibrium constant are listed below:

$$CaF_{2(s)} \leftrightarrow Ca^{2+}{}_{(aq)} + 2\ F^{-}{}_{(aq)} \qquad K_{sp} = [Ca^{2+}][F^{-}]^2$$

The completed checkbook is listed below for excess $CaF_{2(s)}$ dissolved in water.

Species	Ca^{2+}	2 F^-
initial	0 M	0 M
Δ	$+x$	$+2x$
equilibrium	$+x$	$+2x$

Note that 2 moles of F^- are produced for every 1 mole of $CaF_{2(s)}$ that undergoes dissociation. If we enter these values into the equilibrium expression we obtain:

$$K_{sp} = [x][2x]^2$$

and with K_{sp} being $= 3.9 \times 10^{-11}$ (from the Appendix of your textbook.)

$$3.9 \times 10^{-11} = [x][2x]^2$$

To determine the molar solubility, we must rearrange the expression in terms of x. Note that the $2x$ term is squared. We must deal with this term first before we rearrange.

$$3.9 \times 10^{-11} = \left[x \right]\left[4x^2 \right] \qquad \text{(inserting terms)}$$

$$3.9 \times 10^{-11} = \left[4x^3 \right] \qquad \text{(combining terms)}$$

$$\left[x^3 \right] = \frac{3.9 \times 10^{-11}}{4} \qquad \text{(dividing by 4)}$$

$$x = \sqrt[3]{9.8 \times 10^{-12}} \qquad \text{(taking cube root)}$$

$$x = 2.1 \times 10^{-4} \qquad \text{(the molar solubility)}$$

See Sample Exercise 17.11 for another problem concerning the solubility of $CaF_{2(s)}$. Similar problems that involve the calculation of the molar solubility are 17.37, 17.39-17.42. Problems that involve the calculation of the K_{sp} are 17.35, and 17.36, and 17.38.

If you have difficulty taking the cube root of this expression or your calculator does not have a cube root function, see Section 1 of this booklet. Also, while setting up the problem, make sure you have raised all concentrations to the appropriate power before you begin to rearrange the equation and solve for x.

Section 12

Skills for Chapter 19: Thermodynamics

Goals: to calculate entropy, enthalpy, and free energy changes and to calculate the effect of free energy on the equilibrium constant

Skills: multiplication, division, logarithms, and powers

12.1 Enthalpy and Entropy Changes

In Chapter 5 of your text, the concept of enthalpy was presented to you. Each product and reactant in a chemical reaction can be assigned an enthalpy value, $\Delta H°_f$ (found in Appendix C of your text). The change in enthalpy, $\Delta H°_{rxn}$ is calculated by subtracting the sum of the enthalpy values of the reactants from the sum of enthalpy values from the products. The standard entropy change can be calculated in an identical fashion. The $S°$ values for certain species are also listed in Appendix C. Remember, the ° symbol means that all products and reactants involved in the reaction are at standard state (gases at 1 atm pressure, solutions at 1 M, $T = 298$ K).

12.2 Gibb's Free Energy

The change in free energy is defined as:

$$\Delta G° \;=\; \Delta H° \,-\, T\Delta S$$

This $\Delta G°$ term can be calculated by two methods. In Appendix C of your text, $\Delta G°_f$ values are listed. The change in free energy, $\Delta G°_f$ is calculated by subtracting the sum of $\Delta G°_f$ values of the reactants from the sum of $\Delta G°_f$ values of the products. The second method would involve using the $\Delta H°_f$ and $S°$ values for the reaction and the temperature under which the reaction was run. Please note that the units of $\Delta H°_f$ are in kJ/mol while $S°$ values are in J/mol-K. You will need to convert these values to either J or kJ to add them together and find $\Delta G°$.

12.3 Free Energy and Equilibrium

The relationship that is used to relate the $\Delta G°$ and the equilibrium constant is:

$$\Delta G° = -RT \ln K$$

Here R is the gas content (in J/K-mol), T is the temperature in Kelvin. This equation is described in Section 19.7 of your textbook. You will use this equation to determine the equilibrium constant K when the $\Delta G°$ value is given or determined from both tables.

To determine the K value using this equation, it is necessary to take the anti-log of both sides of the equation. This is shown below:

$$e^{\left(\frac{-\Delta G°}{RT}\right)} = e^{\left(\ln K\right)} \qquad \text{(which reduces to)}$$

$$e^{\left(\frac{-\Delta G°}{RT}\right)} = K$$

(Remember, whenever a ln term is used in e^x expression, the two cancel each other out.)

With this relationship, K for a reaction can be found when $\Delta G°$ is known. As an example, let's find K for a reaction where $\Delta G° = -1.23$ kJ and the temperature is 23°C. Before entering the data into the equation, the values must be listed in the appropriate units.

$$
\begin{array}{rcl}
\Delta G° &=& -12,300 \text{ J} \\
T &=& 296 \text{ K} \\
R &=& 8.314 \text{ J/K-mol}
\end{array}
$$

Now, substituting into the equation:

$$e^{\left(\frac{-(-12,300)}{8.314 \times 296}\right)} = K$$

$$e^{(4.998)} = K \qquad (\text{using the } e^x \text{function})$$

$$K = 148$$

Sample Exercise 19.11 in your textbook shows another example of this type of calculation for determining K. See Problems 19.61-19.62 for similar problems.

Another type of calculation that you may encounter is the determining of $\Delta G°$ if you are given the K, and T. For instance, calculate $\Delta G°$ for a reaction which has a K of 2.0×10^3 at 25°C. Substitute this information into the formula and write:

$$\Delta G° = -(8.314 \text{ J/K-mol}) (298 \text{ K}) (\ln 2.0 \times 10^3)$$

(and simplifying)

$$\Delta G° = -(8.314 \text{ J/K-mol} (298 \text{ K}) (7.60)$$
$$\Delta G° = -1.88 \times 10^4 \text{ J} \quad \text{or} \quad -18.8 \text{ kJ}$$

Use this equation to solve Problems 19.65 and 19.66.

Section 13
Skills for Chapter 20: Electrochemistry

Goals: to calculate K values based on cell potentials, to calculate cell potentials using Nernst equation, and to calculate the amount of metals deposited during electrolysis

Skills: multiplication, division, logarithms

13.1 emf, K, and the Nernst equation

An electrochemical cell contains reactants and products that are undergoing a chemical reaction. As we have learned in the previous chapter, the concentration of products and reactants in a chemical reaction at equilibrium can be expressed through the use of the equilibrium constant and equilibrium expression. In Chapter 20 of your textbook, the authors have shown you new equations that relate the cell potential (E) to the free energy change (ΔG), and the reaction quotient (Q) to ΔG. Through substitution of these two relationships, equation 20.15 of your textbook was obtained. The equation is called the *Nernst equation* and is shown below:

$$E = E^\circ - \frac{2.30RT}{nF} \log Q$$

Here R is the gas constant (8.314 J/K-mol), T is the temperature in K, n is the number of electrons involved in the reaction, F is the Faradaic constant of 96,500 J/V-mol. You may note that the equation has several constants. We can simplify this equation by reducing (R/F) to one number. To make the expression even simpler, reactions run at room temperature (298K) allow us to factor in the temperature, T. Also we can place the ln-log conversion term of 2.303. Hence, we may reduce (2.303 RT/F) to a value of 0.0592 V. (Note the unit of the reduced terms in is volts.)

$$E = E^\circ - \frac{0.0592 \text{ V}}{n} \log Q \qquad (T = 298 \text{ K})$$

You will be asked to use this expression to calculate E for a chemical reaction. For instance, let's say a chemical reaction possessed a Q of 5.0×10^{-10} and a $E°$ of 0.25 V. Also, the reaction involved a 1 electron transfer ($n = 1$). Based on this information, E can be calculated with the above formula:

$$E = E° - \frac{0.0592 \text{ V}}{1} \log (5.0 \times 10^{-10})$$

$$E = 0.25° - 0.0592 \times (-9.30)$$

$$E = 0.25 \text{ V} - (-0.55 \text{ V})$$

$$E = 0.80 \text{ V}$$

Sample Exercise 20.11 is similar to this worked example.

A good example of how to use the Nernst Equation can be seen in the determination of cell potential of a "Cu/Zn" battery at $25.0°C$. The redox reaction is:

$$Zn^0{}_{(s)} + Cu^{2+}{}_{(aq)} \leftrightarrow Zn^{2+}{}_{(aq)} + Cu^0{}_{(s)}$$

We can determine that $E° = 1.10$ V from the standard reduction tables and $n = 2$. If we are told that the $(Cu^{2+}) = 0.20$M and $(Zn^{2+}) = 0.80$M, the calculation can be started. First, let's determine Q. The expression for Q in this reaction is:

$$Q = \frac{(Zn^{2+})}{(Cu^{2+})}$$

The Q expression will only be concerned with the concentration of those species in solution. The solid Zn and Cu (the electrodes) do not have a concentration and are not involved in the calculation of Q (for reference, see Chapter 15 of your textbook). Using the solution data we find:

$$Q = \frac{(0.80)}{(0.20)} = 4.0$$

Entering these data into the Nernst equation, we write:

$$E = 1.10 \text{ V} - \left(\frac{0.0592 \text{ V}}{2}\right) \times \log 4.0$$

$$E = 1.10 \text{ V} - \left(\frac{0.0592 \text{ V}}{2}\right) \times (0.602)$$

$$E = 1.10 \text{ V} - (0.296 \text{ V}) \times (0.602)$$

$$E = 1.08 \text{ V}$$

If you are given concentrations of the products and reactants in the redox equations and you know the temperature, you can calculate the cell potential. Of course, you have to be able to write the balanced redox equation. This step is most crucial, since the Q expression and n value are dependent on the stoichiometry of the balanced redox reaction.

Additional problems are found in the end of Chapter 20 for the Nernst equation. Problems 20.51-20.54 and 20.58 are similar to the example shown above. Problems 20.55-20.56 are variants of these problems in that you are asked to find the concentrations of products or reactants based upon a given E value.

In many situations we may wish to determine the value of the equilibrium constant K rather than Q. This can be accomplished by knowing that at equilibrium $\Delta G° = 0$ and therefore, $E = 0$ for a reaction. (Remeber, $\Delta G° = -nFE$.) We can substitute this information into the above equation and find:

$$0 = E° - \frac{0.0592}{n} \log K \qquad \text{(substituting values)}$$

$$E° = \frac{0.0592}{n} \log K \qquad \text{(rearranging)}$$

$$\log K = \frac{nE^\circ}{0.0592} \qquad \text{(solving for } K)$$

As we have seen earlier, to solve for K we must take the anti-log (*10^x* of both sides of the equation). Doing so generates the following equation:

$$K = 10^{\left(\frac{n E^\circ}{0.0592}\right)}$$

As an example, consider a reaction where $n = 2$ and $E^\circ = 1.00$. The value of K is calculated as follows:

$$K = 10^{\left(\frac{2 \times 1.00}{0.0592}\right)}$$

$$K = 10^{(33.78)}$$

$$K = 6.1 \times 10^{33} \qquad \text{(by using } 10^x)$$

Sample Exercise 20.14 demonstrates the use of this equation to find K for a reaction. This solution is accomplished by first balancing the reaction (to find the value of n) and calculating E°. With these data, K can be calculated.

You may also be asked to calculate E° if given the K value. Enter the data into the formula, (with care to use the *log* button and not *ln*) for the determination of K. Also, see if the temperature of the reaction is 298 K (25°C).

See Problems 20.59 and 20.60 for more problems on the calculation of K. Problems 20.61 and 20.62 explore the effect of n on K.

13.2 Electrolysis

An important application of electrochemistry is electrolysis, sometimes known as electroplating. Because the chemical reaction used in this process is based on a reduction reaction, the monitoring of the moles of electrons passed through the reaction vessel, will inform us as to the number of moles of material plated on the electrodes. To determine the number of moles of electrons, the number of amperes (A) is multiplied by the number of seconds of current flow and then divided by F (Faraday's constant).

$$n_{e^-} = \frac{A \times e}{F}$$

After obtaining the n_{e^-} value, the stoichiometry of the reduction equation will allow us to see the theoretical mole quantity of metal that would be deposited on the molecular weight of the metal.

Sometimes the electrolysis reactions take several minutes to hours to perform. This time value is greatly dependent upon the A used. Therefore, take care in working these problems that all time values are converted to s.

See Sample Exercises 20.17 and 20.18 for worked problems on electrolysis. Problems 20.81-21.84, 20.87 and 20.88 are similar to these examples.

Section 14

Skills for Chapter 21: Nuclear Chemistry

Goals: to determine the half-life of a radioactive element
Skills: multiplication, division, logarithms, exponential notation

In this chapter you will work problems concerning the decay of radioactive elements. This decay process follows first order kinetics. The equations are:

$$\ln \frac{N_t}{N_0} = -kt \qquad \text{(decay equation)}$$

$$k = \frac{0.693}{t_{1/2}} \qquad \text{(half-life equation)}$$

To illustrate the use of these equations, consider the medical application of radioactive tracers that are used to monitor illnesses in patients. If a certain tracer has a half-life of 30.0 minutes, how much of a 1.00 mg sample of the tracer would still be active after 45.0 minutes?

First, let us determine k. From the half-life data and the equation:

$$k = \frac{0.693}{30.0 \text{ min}}$$

$$k = 0.0231 \text{ min}^{-1}$$

If N_0 was 4.00 mg and with this value of k, we use the decay equation to solve for the remaining mass of the tracer at $t = 45.0$ min, $N_{45.0}$:

$$\ln \frac{N_{45.0}}{4.00 \text{ mg}} = -(0.0231 \text{ min}^{-1}) \times (45.0 \text{ min})$$

$$\ln \frac{N_{45.0}}{4.00 \text{ mg}} = -1.039$$

$$\frac{N_{45.0}}{4.00 \text{ mg}} = e^{-1.039} \qquad \text{(using } e^x \text{ to remove } ln \text{ term)}$$

$$\frac{N_{45.0}}{4.00 \text{ mg}} = 0.3536$$

$$N_{45.0} = 1.41 \text{ mg}$$

Sample Exercises 21.7 and 21.8 in your textbook are similar to this problem. Problems 21.29 and 21.30 are also similar to these exercises. Problems 21.31-21.34 ask you to calculate $t_{1/2}$ based upon given information of N_t and N_0. Finally the half-life equation is used in Problems 21.37-21.40 to determine the age of a sample based upon N_t and N_0 and $t_{1/2}$.

Section 15
Self Test for Math Skills

Listed below are a series of questions designed to check your math skills. Please take no more than 30 minutes in answering them. You will find the answers and an assessment chart in the back of this booklet.

1. How many significant figures are in the number 0.101?

2. Solve for x in the following equation with care to express the correct number of significant figures.

$$x = 12.011 + 1.00797$$

3. Solve for x in the following equation with care to express the correct number of significant figures.

$$x = \frac{1.057}{10.3}$$

4. Express the number 0.000356 in scientific notation.

5. Determine the mean, $\bar{x}$, for the following data: 25.12, 25.29, 24.95, 25.05 and 25.55.

6. Solve the equation: $x = 2.0\,(\sin 35°)$.

7. Solve the equation: $0.405 = \cos(x)$.

8. Determine the value of x in the following equation.

$$(20.3) \times (0.0171) = \left(\frac{x}{60.3}\right) \times (1.35 \times 10^3)$$

9. What percentage of 15.5 is 1.25?

10. Solve the following equation for x.

$$\frac{1}{x} = \frac{4.3}{6.8}$$

11. Solve the following equation for x.

$$\frac{0.57}{0.22} = \frac{1.2}{x^2}$$

12. Calculate the value of x, where $x = (6.23 \times 1.22)^3$.

13. What is the fourth root of 17?

14. Solve the following equation for x.

$$x = 8.3 \times \left(\frac{1}{2^2} - \frac{1}{4^2}\right)$$

15. Determine the value of x in the following equation.

$$2.52 = \sqrt{\frac{1}{x}}$$

16. Calculate the value of x, where $x = \log(0.017)$.

17. Find the value of x, where $x = e^{\ln(12)}$.

18. Determine the value of x, where $1.53 = \log(x)$.

19. Solve for x in the following equation.

$$x = \frac{-1}{0.030} \times \ln\left(\frac{0.20}{0.50}\right)$$

20. Solve for x in the following equation.

$$x = \left(1.00 \times 10^3\right) e^{\left(\frac{-0.0220}{1.33}\right)}$$

Section 16
Chemistry & Writing

16.1 The Scientific Notebook

The scientific notebook is the scientist's own record of experiments performed and phenomena observed. Beginning with the first student laboratory report there are special requirements for recording experimental results. The requirements may seem rigid at first, but they are very understandable in the light of the purposes of the notebook.

For the professional scientist the claim to original work is found in the scientific notebook. Millions of dollars in patent rights may depend on the existence of a properly dated and authenticated scientific notebook. Many of the rules that are followed in recording data follow from this important function of the notebook. Nothing is ever erased; and incorrect reading is crossed out and the correct one written beside it. Work is recorded in a bound notebook with pages that cannot be removed or added. Every entry is dated, signed, and countersigned by the scientist in charge of the laboratory. All these rules are designed to produce a record that will constitute proof not only of what experiments were performed, but of the exact date. This is important, because if two scientists make the same discovery, the first one to do so will gain all the legal rights and most of the credit for the work. Obviously, it is more important to have a complete and original record than a perfectly neat one. A few crossed-out readings are not uncommon, and a few blots from spilled chemicals are not unheard of either. These are preferable in the laboratory notebook to a perfect page that has been copied over at a later date and no longer constitutes an authentic original record. **Under no circumstances is data to be recorded on loose paper rather than directly into the notebook!**

Another important function of the notebook is to record the procedure and observations so clearly and completely that the experiment can easily be repeated at a later date. Experiments that cannot be repeated by the same researcher or by other laboratories are soon discredited. For the student in the laboratory complete notes are important as well. If something goes wrong, it should be possible to find the error in procedure from the experiment notes. At times, the numbers in the crossed-out data entries tell an interesting story. Occasionally an interesting and unexpected phenomenon will be observed that merits further study. Always a complete, clear record of what has happened in the laboratory is essential.

In order to be a complete record, each experiment entered into the notebook should include certain features. The scientist's **name** and the **date** should always be entered. The **title of the experiment** being performed is an important element that is often neglected. "Chemistry Lab" is an inadequate substitute for the experiment title, which is usually readily available. Often it is useful to begin by writing the **objective**, or the purpose, of the experiment. Stating the objective clearly helps both the experimenter and the reader of the notebook to understand the experiment. A complete record of experimental **procedure** is essential, either as a step-by-step description or by a complete reference to a standard experimental procedure. If a standard procedure is given, great care must be made to note any deviations from that procedure. A list of **materials and equipment** used can be a great help in organization if it is included as a part of the experimental procedure.

Though the laboratory notebook does not have to be perfectly pristine, it is certainly desirable that it should be as organized as possible. Some time and thought spent in planning before the laboratory period begins will result in a better notebook and a more successful experiment. **The date, title, experimenter's name and objective of the experiment should be entered before the experiment begins.** If the experimental procedure that has been provided does not already give **labeled data tables** for an experiment, it is worth some time and thought to set up such tables before entering the laboratory, rather than waste time during the experiment deciding how to do so. Ample space should be provided not only for the expected data, but also for corrections and notes. Unused space can be crossed out later as necessary, though extra pages are never torn out. Sometimes only the right-hand pages of the notebook are used, leaving the other pages free for later notes or calculations. Individual research laboratories or student laboratories may have standard notebooks or forms in which to write laboratory results. All of them share the basic objective of recording in a useful way the scientist's actions, observations, and thoughts while in the laboratory.

16.2 The Scientific Report

When the scientist makes a formal written report of experiments performed in the laboratory, the report follows a generally accepted outline. Introduction, results and discussion, conclusions follow in order as separate sections and are clearly labeled. Lists of references and even the title are treated in standard ways.

The **title** of a scientific paper is seldom an occasion for creativity. Titles for articles in scientific journals are carefully constructed from words that will be useful key words for information searches by computer. Titles for student laboratory reports are usually indicated in the assignment. As with the laboratory notebook, "Chemistry Laboratory" is unacceptably vague as a laboratory report title. Abbreviations as part of a title should be avoided.

The **Introduction** section should make clear to the reader the purpose and the background of the experiment. The objective of the work that is being discussed should always be clearly stated. It may be appropriate to discuss the basis of the experimental methods that were used as well as the scientific theory on which the work is based. Usually a well-written introduction makes use of written resources in the form of scientific books and papers, which must be listed in the references cited and footnoted with the appropriate reference.

The **Experimental Procedure** section explains in detail exactly how the experiment was conducted. It should be possible to reproduce the experiment using the information found in this section. If standard procedures are used and not explained in detail, a reference should be given. A list of materials and equipment is often a useful component in this section. It includes all chemicals used, including the concentrations of solutions, and all special equipment.

The **Results and Discussion** section includes the data that were obtained in the experiment together with an explanation of the data. Often it is useful to organize the results of the experiment in tables, and sometimes graphs are required as well. All tables and figures should be titled and numbered. All columns in tables and both axes of a graph should be carefully labeled, not omitting units. If calculations have been performed, the equations used should be clearly indicated and enough information about the calculations should be included so that they can be clearly followed. The precision and accuracy of the results should be calculated by standard statistical methods if appropriate to the experiment.

The **Conclusions** section contains the thoughts of the experimenter about the significance of the work performed. Each part of the experiment should be discussed. Numerical results should be evaluated, and the meaning of any statistical calculations explained. The success of the experiment should be evaluated by referring to the objective of the experiment as presented in the introduction. Was the experiment successful? Were the objectives met? What is the overall significance of the experiment?

The **Literature Cited** section lists all the references used in preparing the report. This section is most formalized of all in its format. Each scientific journal has a slightly different style which contributors must follow to the letter. Student reports may also be required to follow a certain form. The best way to write this section is with the help of an example. Often college courses use scientific journals as models. The *Journal of Chemical Education, Analytical Chemistry* and the *Journal of the American Chemical Society* are examples of chemical journals which have been used in this way; the *Journal of Organic Chemistry* is often used in organic chemistry courses. When giving references it is important to notice carefully all words that are set in italics or boldface in the example references. Typesetters use different fonts for italics and boldface that are difficult to reproduce when typing or handwriting, though many word processing programs are able to reproduce them. Words that are set in **italics can be indicated by an underline. Boldface can be represented by a wavy underline.** Typically, a reference to a book appears as follows:

REID, R. C.; SHERWOOD, T. K.; PRAUSNITZ, J. M. *Properties of Gases and Liquids*; McGraw Hill: New York, 1977.

A reference to a scientific journal follows this general form:

LEE, L. G.; WHITESIDES, G. M. *J. Am. Chem. Soc.* **1985**, *107*, 6999.

16.3 Technical Writing

Scientific writing is not limited to scientific journal articles. Scientists on every level are more likely to achieve success if they are able to describe their work and explain its significance to others. Technical writing can vary from a brief explanation of how to use a piece of equipment to a lengthy report on the activities in the laboratory. Technical writers produce articles written for the layman explaining technical subjects in understandable terms. Effective technical writing is a job skill that is very much in demand. College-level assignments that involve report-writing on technical subjects require the same considerations as professional writing.

First, consider the audience. Will the material be read by a skilled professional or a layman? If it cannot be assumed that the reader is familiar with the basic principles of the field being discussed, then the writing must include some basic background information, with special attention given to explaining technical vocabulary that may not be understood by the reader.

Most writing projects begin with a visit to the library to find appropriate source materials. Again, the level of the project will determine how the literature search is conducted. The original research reports contained in scientific journals can be found through indexes such as those provided in *Chemical Abstracts*; using the abstract indexes is a skill that must be developed through practice. Chemistry students usually are given a special course in the chemical literature that includes training in the use of *Chemical Abstracts*. Many science reports, however, require only limited use of original research papers. Science encyclopedias and dictionaries, along with periodicals written for the layman, can provide the background information for a science report and may indicate as well the authors and topics that might be explored in a more detailed technical search. Science and technology encyclopedias useful as sources of background information include:

Harper Encyclopedia of Science
McGraw-Hill Encyclopedia of Science and Technology
Van Nostrand's Scientific Encyclopedia

More specialized encyclopedias include:

Encyclopedia of Chemical Technology
Encyclopedia of Physics
McGraw-Hill Encyclopedia of Energy

Dictionaries can be useful in defining technical terms and concepts. Those that are useful in chemistry-related topics include:

Chamber's Dictionary of Science and Technology (McGraw-Hill)
Chemist's Dictionary (Van Nostrand)
Hanckh's Chemical Dictionary (McGraw-Hill)
McGraw-Hill Dictionary of Scientific and Technical Terms

Facts and data can be found through the many scientific handbooks. Some of the handbooks used in researching chemistry papers include:

CRC Handbook of Biochemistry
CRC Handbook of Chemistry and Physics
CRC Handbook of Environmental Control
Merck Index

Review articles in periodicals like *Scientific American* give useful information on a variety of scientific topics. They can be conveniently found through the *General Science Index*, which provides a comprehensive subject index to English language periodical literature in the sciences. On-line computer search services are increasingly used to locate periodical references. A major resource of the library not to be neglected is the expertise of a good science librarian.

Technical writing depends no less than any other form of writing on the basic language skills of the writer. Incorrect spelling and grammar can mar the effect of the most interesting and original narrative. A good guide to English usage belongs next to a dictionary on the writer's desk. Good writing style is developed through practice in writing and rewriting. A clear, direct style contains no unnecessary words. Consider the following example:

```
At this point in the experiment the mixture was
heated up through the use of a hotplate.
```

A much improved version is:

```
The mixture was heated with a hotplate.
```

Some science publications prefer that use of the first person ("I heated the mixture") be avoided. Use of the passive voice "the mixture was heated" is then indicated. In other uses the more direct form of the active voice may be preferred, as in, "We decided to heat the mixture" rather than, "It was decided that the mixture should be heated." When writing instructions the imperative is often a good choice: "Heat the mixture on a hot plate" is more direct than "The mixture should be heated on a hot plate."

There are many references available to you to help you develop the valuable skill of communicating information. General references include:

W. STRUNK, Jr.; E. B. WHITE. *The Elements of Style,* Macmillan: New York, 1979.

MARGARET SHERTZER. *The Elements of Grammar,* Macmillan: New York, 1986.

References pertaining to technical information are:

B. EDWARD CAIN. *The Basics of Technical Communicating*; American Chemical Society: Washington, DC, 1988.

ANNE EISENBERG. *Writing Well for the Technical Professions*; Harper and Row: New York, 1989.

16.4 A Notebook Example

The following three pages illustrate the proper manner in which a laboratory notebook should be kept. These pages are reproductions of a student's analytical chemistry laboratory notebook. The style of this notebook conforms to the guidelines presented in Section 16.1 of this booklet.

Before entering the laboratory the student had written the introduction and experimental section. A section of data/results was begun as the student collected information. (Note that the student recorded the weights of several tablets as well as the time required to complete the coulometric titration of the ascorbic acid tablets). This entry is reproduced on page 89.

Next, the student was required to perform several calculations with these data. They were begun in the laboratory and are found on the next page (p. 90). (Note that this page is the reverse page of the data entry. It would be the left hand page of the notebook.) Normally, the right hand side of the notebook is used for data entry and analysis, while the left hand side is used for "scratch" calculations. This method eliminates the need for "loose" paper for initial calculations and other scribbles.

The last page (p. 91) contains the conclusions. Note that the student corrected the calculated values and his grammar by drawing a line through the unwanted entry. Erasure or correction fluid was not used.

This simple system of using the different sides of the notebook for formal entries and simple calculations can greatly enhance your ability to organize your data and to present your findings.

Coulometric Titration of Ascorbic Acid with Iodine   26 Oct 98

<u>Introduction</u> · The purpose of this experiment is to determine the weight percent of ascorbic acid in a vitamin tablet.

<u>Experimental</u>: Add 0.1M KI solution and a spatula of soluble starch. Cautiously add 1sec increments to the current until a pale blue color appears. This will be the matching color.
Crush a vitamin tablet and weigh 20 to 30 mg to the nearest 0.1mg; transfer to the cell. Turn on current.
Repeat the procedure with 2 more samples from the tablet. Continue to analyze other tablets.

<u>Data/Results</u>: multiplier 0.5 0.05 = 48.25mA
250mg tablets / 361g^{mg} tablet #1, 364.8 tablet^{mg} #2

sample	1	0.0232g tablet	389.2 sec
	2	0.0225g	368.4 sec
	3	0.0243g	—
	4	0.0249g	385.0
	5	0.0240g	359.1
	6	0.0234g	353.0
	7	0.0240g	366.3

Actual Weight	Time	AB Ascorbic Acid		Weight %
0.0232g	389.2sec	0.0171g	} Tablet 1	73.7
0.0225g	368.4sec	0.0162g		72.0
0.0249g	385.0sec	0.0170g		68.3
0.0240g	359.1sec	0.0158g	} Tablet 2	65.8
0.0234g	353.0sec	0.0155g		66.2
0.0240g	366.3sec	0.0161g		67.1

Tablet #1 contained on average 263.0 ± 4.3 mg ascorbic acid.
Tablet #2 contained on average 244., ± 4.2 mg ascorbic acid.

263.0 ± 4.3

244.1 ± 4.2

$$95\% \ CL = \bar{x} \pm \frac{ts}{\sqrt{N}}$$

$$= 263.0 \pm \frac{12.7(4.3)}{\sqrt{2}} \qquad = 244.1 \pm \frac{3.18(4.2)}{\sqrt{2} \ 4}$$

$$= 263 \pm 38 \qquad = 244.1 \pm 9.4$$
$$6.7$$

$$\bar{x} - \mu = 263 - 250 \qquad \frac{ts}{\sqrt{N}} = \frac{(12.7)(4.3)}{\sqrt{2}}$$

$$= +13 \qquad = \pm 38$$

$$\bar{x} - \mu = 244 - 250 \qquad \frac{ts}{\sqrt{N}} = 6.7$$

$$= 6$$

<u>Conclusion</u>: The value given on the box for each ascorbic acid tablet was 250 mg. We The obtained results for two tablets were $263._0 \pm 4.3$ mg and $244._1 \pm 4.2$ mg. The results are close to the reported value. Some error can be expected in this experiment because the calculations depend on an observed endpoint, and although it is tried, it is sometimes hard to pick the same endpoint each time based on color.

The third run on the first tablet was discarded because the electrode was not in the solution and therefore no reaction was taking place.

The 95% CI produces results of 263 ± 38 for the first tablet, which rounds to $26_3 \pm 3_8$. This is mainly high because it is based on two readings. The second tablet gave a result of $244._1 \pm 9._{\text{7}}$ mg. This is based on four readings.

A t-test on the first tablet gives $+38 < +13$, which says that our result is good and would, on average, be correct 95 of 100 times. Our second tablet gives $-6.7 < 6$, which suggests that our second value can also be accepted.

The overall reliability of Coulometric titrations is good as long as you pick an endpoint and can reproduce it.

Section 17
Chemistry & Career Planning

C hemists often find themselves in careers that seem unrelated to traditional chemistry, yet draw heavily on chemical knowledge and skills. Some chemists go into management; management positions in science-related industries are expected to increase 30% by the year 2000. Technical sales, patent law, and forensic science are only a few of the careers open to holders of chemistry degrees. Laboratory workers are needed in materials science, polymers, and biotechnology; all these fields depend on the molecular science of chemistry. The traditional skills of chemical analysis and synthesis are in demand for such areas as environmental testing and pharmaceutical development. A wide variety of rewarding career options are available for those with chemical training. The overall unemployment rate for chemists is very low, averaging about 1%.

17.1 Materials Science

One of the major predicted growth areas in the economy is in the area of materials science. The new superconducting materials that promise major breakthrough applications in fields as diverse as communications and transportation are the product of materials science. The development of new graphite materials is resulting in new types of tennis rackets, aircraft, and auto bodies. New ceramic materials are being researched for a variety of uses, including automotive pollution control. Fiber optic materials are revolutionizing communications.

Like many of the fields that offer exciting new job opportunities, materials science is interdisciplinary, requiring a knowledge of chemistry and physics. The field employs both chemists and chemical engineers. Courses in polymer science, metallurgy, and computer science are also helpful. Industry employs the largest number of materials scientists: government and university positions are possible in this field as well.

17.2 Polymer Science

The long-chain giant molecules called polymers form a special class of materials that find a wide variety of uses. Synthetic fibers like nylons and polyesters are the basis of a major industry. Packaging materials as diverse as Saran Wrap and Styrofoam are made of polymers. Televisions, computers, toys, tapes, and CDs all make use of polymeric materials. Increasing concern about solid waste disposal is prompting research on plastic recycling and degradability. A promising research area involves modification of polymer properties to make materials that will be compatible with human tissues for medical transplants. Preparation for an industrial career in polymer science may involve a degree in chemistry, chemical engineering, or polymer science and engineering.

17.3 Environmental Science and Technology

Increasing concern about the environment has created numerous job openings for scientists who want to find solutions to the problems caused by pollution. Understanding the chemical and biochemical reactions that produce and consume chemicals like carbon dioxide and methane in the atmosphere is critical to understanding the possible long-range warming process known as the greenhouse effect. Chemists discovered that the chemical reactions of CFC's, or compounds containing carbon, fluorine, and chlorine, with ozone in the upper atmosphere, were causing ozone depletion and a resultant increase in the amount of harmful ultraviolet radiation that is reaching the earth's surface. Now chemists must discover substitutes for these compounds that will replace them in such uses as refrigerants for refrigerators and air conditioners. Automobiles and factories must be designed so that their combustion processes do not foul the air. Factory effluent must be treated or recycled so that streams and groundwater are not polluted.

State and federal agencies such as the Environmental Protection Agency employ chemists to monitor pollution and help to find ways to decrease its sources. Waste management companies recycle materials or dispose of them responsibly, an increasingly technical task.

Chemists, biochemists, and chemical engineers all find employment in areas of environmental technology.

17.4 Biochemistry and Biotechnology

Biochemists study the chemistry of living systems. Understanding the reactions which occur in the human body, in animals, plants, insects, viruses, and microorganisms makes possible new approaches to curing disease and improving food technology. Unlocking the human genetic code is the aim of the human genome project currently underway; its implication for our society will be profound. Colleges and universities employ almost half the biochemistry workforce; the rest are employed by government agencies or private companies.

Biotechnology is a burgeoning new interdisciplinary field employing biochemists, chemists, and biologists. Most of these are employed in industry, either by established pharmaceutical and agricultural companies or by new biotechnology venture firms in this rapidly growing area. Through biotechnology, scientific breakthroughs in molecular biology are used to develop new products for the commercial marketplace. Microorganisms are being produced on a large scale which are able to produce insulin or the human growth hormone. Specific microorganisms are being produced with the goal of consuming oil spills or hazardous chemical waste. Genetic variation of plants may produce varieties which are richer in nutrients or resistant to insects. These are but the beginnings of the commercial applications which may be expected in biotechnology.

17.5 Medicinal Chemistry and Clinical Chemistry

Biochemistry and biotechnology are improving both our understanding of diseases and the methods of treatment, but they are not the only fields of chemistry related to medicine. Medicinal chemistry and clinical chemistry are specialties in which chemists have a direct impact on health care.

The medicinal chemist develops new therapeutic agents. Chemical compounds are designed and synthesized with the aim of producing molecules which will act on one area of the body, such as a certain part of the brain. Once the compound has been synthesized, it is ready for the long series of tests for both positive and harmful effects which all new drugs must undergo. Tests may indicate that further modification of the molecule's structure is required. Preparation for this work, which links chemistry, biology, and medicine, requires training in chemistry, pharmacology, or medicinal chemistry.

The clinical chemist applies the techniques of analytical chemistry to body fluids. A variety of chemical instrumentation is used, and the modern clinical laboratory makes extensive use of computer automated testing. Administrative duties may form an important part of the clinical chemist's work. Clinical tests are performed both to monitor normal body functions and to test for therapeutic and toxic drug levels in the body. Often critical decisions about health care are based on laboratory results. Many clinical laboratories are involved in research-related testing, to find the results of new procedures, drugs, and equipment or to support basic research. Clinical chemists are employed by hospitals, universities, government and industry.

17.6 Forensic Science

Forensic chemists apply the skills of analytical chemistry in the crime laboratory. Suspected samples of drugs must be analyzed for authenticity by chemical instrumentation if they are used as legal evidence. Body fluids and samples of body tissue are provided by the medical examiner for analysis in the case of a homicide, and cases of sexual assault involve laboratory testing as well. Traces of blood or of gunshot residue can be revealed by chemical tests. Other skills are required of the general forensic scientist, such as investigation of the crime scene. Though these are not directly related to chemistry, some of the most eminent forensic scientists were trained as chemists. Most forensic scientists are employed by government laboratories.

17.7 Radiochemistry

An exciting area of chemistry which is experiencing severe shortages of trained workers is radiochemistry. This specialty is needed in a multitude of application areas, some of which are growing rapidly.

Nuclear medicine is seeing rapid advances in such areas as the use of monoclonal antibodies in cancer research. The radiopharmaceutical industry needs radiochemists both to manufacture radionuclides and to oversee waste disposal and protection from radiation hazard. Positron emission tomography (PET) is a new diagnostic application of radio-pharmacology which requires radiochemists to staff PET centers and to develop and provide radionuclides and labeled compounds. PET is expected to expand rapidly as its use shifts from primarily research use to more routine medical applications.

Nuclear power production requires radiochemists both in power plants and in related industries to oversee the running of plants and to supervise waste treatment.

Environmental chemistry makes use of radiochemistry in several ways. Accidental emissions from power plants such as the Chernobyl accident require skilled monitoring to assess environmental and health effects. Radionuclides can be used as tags to monitor complex systems such as the buildup of greenhouse gases or the sources of atmospheric CFC's which destroy the ozone layer. Neutron activation analysis can analyze for trace elements in rocks and help explain earth's history.

17.8 Patent Attorneys and Patent Agents

A background in chemistry can serve as preparation for the career of patent attorney or patent agent. A patent attorney must have a law degree as well as a science degree. A patent agent may have a degree in chemistry, physics, engineering, or related technological fields. For certification the patent agent must pass an examination on patent procedures and rules. The patent agent examines the patent literature to determine whether a client's invention is patentable and writes patent applications. Patent lawyers may in addition represent a client in litigation on licensing, trademark or copyright issues, trade secrets cases, and antitrust cases. Patent agent and attorneys are always well-paid and in short supply. Their work involves communication skills as well as scientific training. They are in demand both by government offices and private law firms.

17.9 Chemical Education

Chemistry is taught at both the high school and the college level. College chemistry is taught at two-year and four-year colleges and at universities. Teaching positions at larger universities are likely to involve greater emphasis on graduate education and research than on undergraduate instruction. Demand for high-school teachers has lessened temporarily for demographic reasons, as the number of high school students has decreased. Increasing elementary school enrollments indicate this trend will be short-lived.

Teachers at all levels speak of the satisfactions involved in interacting with young minds and influencing future careers. Individual freedom is often greater than in many other types of employment, and scheduling is more flexible. College professors have many obligations in addition to teaching, however. Committee responsibilities are required as a part of participation in college governance, and administrative duties may be part of some professor's workloads. Research involves not only study and planning, but also the training of graduate students and postdoctoral fellows and the writing of proposals for research funding. Financial rewards may not be as great as those of the industrial chemist, especially at the high school level and at smaller higher education institutions. For those who teach, the quality of life in the work experience is often a major part of the reward.

17.10 Chemical Information Careers

Chemical information is produced at an increasingly rapid rate as new discoveries are made and the results published in scientific journals. Several career possibilities are available to the chemist who can help others to locate and understand the relevant chemical information for their needs.

The chemical information specialist is familiar with both the chemical literature and the on-line computer services through which chemical information is increasingly accessed. Libraries use chemical information specialists, but chemical companies need them also to help their researchers. Often toxicological and environmental information is needed as well as experimental data retrieval. This special kind of problem-solving expertise should remain in demand as information retrieval becomes an increasingly complex field.

Abstracting services summarize and index chemical discoveries so they can be found by their researchers. They employ chemists to prepare information both for written abstract material and for on-line search services.

Science writers are needed on all levels, both to edit and write scientific publications for the scientists and to interpret scientific information in terms the general public can understand. Research organizations, medical centers, technical companies, and government agencies all need writers who can communicate clearly with a variety of audiences. In addition to print media, radio and television employ experts in science communication.

17.11 Other Chemistry Careers

This list of some current options in chemistry careers is by no means complete. Chemists work in museums and metallurgy plants, in food science laboratories and consumer testing services, in adhesives research and photography laboratories. The materials of our modern world are developed by chemists, and chemists monitor the safety of these products and of our environment. The materials of our future and discoveries which will prolong our lives and improve the quality of life will be the product of chemical research.

Section 18
Math Skills Test Answers

answer		*if you missed this problem, refer to:*
1.	3	Section 2.1
2.	13.019	Section 2.1
3.	0.103	Section 2.1
4.	3.56×10^{-4}	Sections 2.2
5.	25.19	Section 2.3
6.	1.1	Section 1.2
7.	66.1°	Section 1.2
8.	0.0155	Section 1.1, 1.2
9.	8.06%	Section 3.1
10.	1.6	Section 1.1, 6.1
11	0.68	Section 1.1, 6.3
12	439	Section 1.3, 1.4
13.	2.03	Section 1.3, 1.4
14.	1.6	Section 5.2
15.	0.157	Section 6.3
16.	-1.77	Sections 1.3, 8.2
17.	12	Sections 1.3, 8.2
18.	34	Sections 1.3, 8.2
19.	31	Section 8.2
20.	984	Section 12.3